]

# Pepsi-Cola

Terry Ravenscroft

# ABOUT THE AUTHOR

The day after Terry Ravenscroft threw in his mundane factory job to become a television comedy scriptwriter he was involved in a car accident which left him unable to turn his head. Since then he has never looked back.

Before they took him away he wrote scripts for Les Dawson, The Two Ronnies, Morecambe and Wise, Alas Smith and Jones, Not the Nine O'Clock News, Ken Dodd, Roy Hudd, and several others. He also wrote the award-winning BBC radio series Star Terk Two.

Born in New Mills, Derbyshire, in 1938, he still lives there with his wife Delma and his mistress Divine Bottom (in his dreams).

# ALSO BY TERRY RAVENSCROFT

STAIRLIFT TO HEAVEN
STAIRLIFT TO HEAVEN 2 - FURTHER UP THE STAIRLIFT
STAIRLIFT TO HEAVEN 3 - ALMOST THERE
STAIRLIFT TO HEAVEN 4 - STILL HANGING ON
CAPTAIN'S DAY
FOOTBALL CRAZY
IT'S NOT CRICKET!
JAMES BLOND - STOCKPORT IS TOO MUCH
INFLATABLE HUGH
I'M IN HEAVEN
DEAR AIR 2000
DEAR COCA-COLA
SAWYER THE LAWYER
LES DAWSON'S CISSIE AND ADA
THE RAZZAMATAZZ FUN EBOOK
ZEPHYR ZODIAC
GOOD OLD GEORGE!
CALL ME A TAXI
DEAD MEN DON'T WALK
THE RING OF THE LORD

# DEAR PEPSI-COLA

****

19 Victoria Gardens
New Mills
High Peak
SK12 4BC

13th January 2015

Customer Care
Starbucks Coffee Company
566 Chiswick High Road
London
W4 5YE

Dear Starbucks

It is not my habit to frequent coffee houses as I much prefer Nescafé. However the other day I found myself in real need of a coffee while in the middle of Manchester, so it was a case of any port in a storm when I called in at your St Ann's Square branch. Unfortunately your counter hand informed that you don't serve Nescafé. This being the case, and faced with a plethora of coffee concoctions none of which I was at all familiar with (and there was no explanation offered), I plumped for a Cappuccino. My wife, equally mystified as to what exactly she would be getting, chose a Latte. I tasted both of them. Both were quite nice. However both, to my taste buds at least, tasted exactly the same. Which leads me to ask: what, if any, is the difference between a Cappuccino and a Latte?

One further question. If Starbucks sees itself as a

classy coffee house - and the outrageous price of its cakes would seem to suggest this - why doesn't it serve Nescafé?

Sincerely

T Ravenscroft (Mr)

STARBUCKS

**Building 4**
**Chiswick Park**
**566 Chiswick High Road**
**London**
**W4 5YE**

Our Ref 17121682

Mr T Ravenscroft
19 Victoria Gardens
New Mills
High Peak
SK12 4BC

30th January 2015

Dear Mr Ravenscroft

Thank you for taking the time to contact Starbucks Coffee Company and visiting one of our stores for the first time.

I am sorry to hear of the confusing and overwhelming experience you had and that the service you received was unhelpful. I can assure you this is not what we would have wanted for your first visit.

Starbucks has always been about creating a comfortable and welcoming environment for our customers, so that they can relax and enjoy themselves in our stores. However our passion has been and will always be about our coffee. Our coffees can range from our Whole Bean freshly brewed coffee, which is always available ready to order, or as you have chosen on your visit, one of our Italian influenced espresso based beverages. These beverages vary in style and can be customised into many different personal drinks.

The difference between a Latte and a Cappuccino is based not on the taste, as we always use 100% Fairtrade Arabica Beans in each beverage, but the style in which it is made. A cappuccino will be made with 1/3 froth to create a creamy but stronger tasting beverage. The latte is made the same but with an inch of foam at the top, creating a milkier coffee.

If you currently enjoy instant styled coffee, I would strongly suggest trying a "Freshly Brewed Coffee" or "American" on your next visit.

Once again thank you for choosing Starbucks and we hope to welcome you back in store soon.

Yours sincerely,

Jonathan S
Customer Care Specialist.

19 Victoria Gardens
New Mills
High Peak
SK12 4BC

13th February 2015

Jonathan S
Starbucks Coffee Company
566 Chiswick High Road
London
W4 5YE

Dear Jonathan S

Thank you for your informative and erudite teach-in on Starbucks' range of coffees. I couldn't help noticing, however, that you carefully avoided the issue of why you don't serve Nescafé. You also conveniently skipped over the question of the outrageous price of your cakes. However...

Visiting London with my wife yesterday I thought I would take the opportunity to give you another try. After taking out a mortgage I bought two of your cakes, which your counter hand served up with a big smile. However the smile immediately disappeared, not to return, when I handed him the jar of Nescafé Gold Blend I had prudently brought along with me and asked if he would trouble himself to make us a couple of cups. He refused point blank. As did your manager. Not only did the manager rebuff this quite reasonable request but when I told him in that case we wouldn't be bothering he refused to take one of the cakes back (although I must admit that my wife had by that time taken a bite out of it). He then had the effrontery to charge me for it. I was so angry that we left immediately, leaving the rest of my wife's Seasonal Twizzle uneaten, at a cost to my wallet of £3.50. And we still hadn't had a coffee!

I am sure it can't be the first time that one of your customers has brought with him a jar of Nescafé and asked you to make him up a cup, or in this case two cups, and would suggest that were you to make Nescafé available in your stores that it would never happen again.

I would appreciate your comments and the reimbursement of my £3.50.

Sincerely
T Ravenscroft (Mr)

STARBUCKS

**Building 4**
**Chiswick Park**
**566 Chiswick High Road**
**London**
**W4 5YE**

**Our Ref 17121682**
Mr T Ravenscroft
19 Victoria Gardens
New Mills
High Peak
SK12 4BC

17th February 2015

Dear Mr Ravenscroft

Thank you for taking the time to contact Starbucks Coffee Company. Providing our customers with premium coffee and great service in a relaxing environment is what our customers expect and appreciate when they visit our stores.

I hope we will have the opportunity to welcome you back into our stores and as a gesture of goodwill I have enclosed two beverage vouchers for you and your wife to enjoy a complimentary drink in one of our stores.

Thank you again for taking the time to share your thoughts with us.

Yours sincerely,

Tracey G, Customer Care Specialist.

19 Victoria Gardens
New Mills
High Peak
SK12 4BC

20th January 2015

Tracey G
Starbucks Coffee Company
566 Chiswick High Road
London
W4 5YE

Dear Tracy G

Thank you for the beverage vouchers. However, giving vouchers for two cups of coffee to someone who doesn't like your coffee is a bit like giving a man who suffers from haemorrhoids another two haemorrhoids, wouldn't you say? Fortunately my next door neighbour doesn't mind your coffee at all so I swapped the vouchers with him for a medium-sized jar of Nescafé.

Sincerely

T Ravenscroft (Mr)

****

19 Victoria Gardens
New Mills
High Peak
SK12 4BC

28th November 2014

Mars
3d Dundee Road
Slough
SL1 4LG

Dear Mars

Last December Mars shrunk the size of its Mars Bars from 58g to 51g, ostensibly to honour their pledge to cut their calorie content to 250 by the end of 2013 in compliance with the Government's Responsibility Deal. However the price of the bar remained the same, which had the effect of yielding approximately an extra 8% profit. People are not dim - as food manufacturers seem to think they are - and this would have been duly noted by many, all of whom no doubt now have less regard for your company than they previously had. This poses the question: 'Is an extra 8% profit worth it, considering the loss of customer goodwill it inevitably brings with it?'

Undoubtedly the Government, before very much longer if I know anything about governments, will be insisting that Mars cut the calorie content of its Mars Bar to 200 calories. How will Mars react to this? My guess is that you will reduce the weight of bars by a degree sufficient to fall in line with this and leave the price unaltered again. Result - the loss of even more customer goodwill. *Which has already been diminished*.

Fortunately I have the answer. The next time you have to reduce the weight of your Mars Bar by, say, 10 %, leave the bar the same weight (and the same price) and simply GET EVERYONE TO PROMISE TO LEAVE 10 PER CENT OF IT! It doesn't matter what they do with the remaining 10 %, they can give it to their dog or cat.

I have tried out this system and found it to it work admirably: for the last month I have provided each of my three sons with a daily Mars Bar with instructions to leave 10% of it and place it in the box provided. This they did, and by the end of the month I had 90 bits of left over Mars Bar. There was not one failure, and my boys love Mars Bars - they sometimes even eat them when they have to pay for them themselves.

There would remain the problem of what to do with the millions of bits of leftover Mars Bar, but if the dog or cat isn't an option they could always be given to the poor.

Sincerely

T Ravenscroft (Mr)

**DUNDEE ROAD**
**SLOUGH**
**SL1 4LG**

09 December 2014

Mr T Ravenscroft
19 Victoria Gardens
New Mills
High Peak
SK12 4BC

**Our ref: 4035/899**

Dear Mr Ravenscroft

Thank you for contacting Mars.

As part of our global commitment to promoting responsible consumption, and as a signatory of the Responsibility Deal's calorie reduction pledge, we made a commitment to ensure that all of our single-serve chocolate products will contain no more than 250 calories per portion by the end of 2013. To meet our commitment, having taken product formulation as far as we can for now without compromising taste, we have reduced the size of Mars Bars.

We believe our products represent good value for money, and we are constantly reinvesting in our products to make them even better.

Thank you for taking the time to contact us. If you need any further information or advice, please contact our Consumer Careline on the telephone number below and one of our Consumer Care Advisors will be more than happy to help you.

Yours sincerely

Lydia Seaton-Read
Consumer Care Team
0845 045 0042

19 Victoria Gardens
New Mills
High Peak
SK12 4BC

16th December 2014

Lydia Seaton-Read
Mars
3d Dundee Road
Slough
SL1 4LG

Dear Lydia Seaton-Read

Thank you for your reply. Unlike your Mars Bars it was neither 10 per cent smaller, nor 10 per cent less evasive and unapologetic, than I expected it to be. However, taking a leaf out of the Mars Book of Getting Away with Giving Less for the Same Price, the rest of this communication will contain 10 per cent fewer letters.

It is no the fist time Mars as droped the weight of Mr Bars while leaving the pric the same. In 2008 it cut he size rom 62.5g to 58g, wile leaving the pric the same, expecting obody in the entire cuntry to notice his. Mrs did jus the same with nickers. So it was a racing certity it wud happen again - I cud have put my shit on it.

Sincerely

T Ravenscroft (Mr)

****

19 Victoria Gardens
New Mills
High Peak
SK12 4BC

20th November 2014

The Cornish Fishmonger
Unit 4, Warren Road
Indian Queens Industrial Estate
Cornwall
TR9 6TL

Dear Cornish Fishmonger

I have recently learned, quite belatedly at my age you might say, that fish is reputed to be good for the brain. I have no reason to dispute this claim; in fact I have very good reason to believe it if the brain power exhibited by my three sons is anything to go by, evidenced as it is by their unsatisfactory performance in the school classroom. So it is probably not a coincidence that for all their lives they have refused to eat fish. On the other hand I have eaten fish twice a week for as long as I can remember and I was a town councillor (Con) by the time I was 30.

Things are about to change, chez Ravenscroft. In an effort to catch up on their non-fish eating years, and hopefully catch up on their lessons, I intend to kick-start my offspring's brains by feeding them fish at least five times a week, whether they like it or not. Well, they won't like it, they have already amply demonstrated that by refusing to eat it; however it is high time I took a stronger line with them before it is too late and, by the time they leave school to make their way in the world, the only path they are equipped to travel leads to a job wearing a funny hat behind the counter at McDonalds, or some other fast food outlet.

Given the above, which fish do you recommend? Are some species of fish better for the brain than others? I ask this as whilst I am keen for my sons to have more brains I don't want to be force feeding them turbot if mackerel is just as good for them, especially as turbot is about three times the price of mackerel; whilst I am not a poor man I don't see the point in paying more than I have to.

Perhaps all types of fish are good for the brain in equal measure? Maybe a mix of fish is the way forward? I would be interested in your comments and possible recommendations.

Sincerely

T Ravenscroft (Mr)

Wing
OF ST MAWES
THE CORNISH
FISHMONGER

25th November 2014

Dear Mr Ravenscroft

I am in receipt of your letter of the 20th instant.

I note your wish to feed the young of your family with fish five times a week. On that basis, might I suggest a wide and varied mix of species be offered as, to offer the same fish time and time again might be counterproductive and produce resistance to your goal?

As to individual species health benefits, I am not qualified to comment. I am sure you are well aware of the well-known benefits of Omega 3 & 6 oils; these are present in all oily fish, such as mackerel, sardine/pilchard, herring and salmon. Likewise crab meat is rich in these oils too. White fish, both flat and round is a good source of protein and delivers around 80 kcals per 100gm portion, having virtually no fat content.

You might well consider including kippers and smoked haddock within your choice of species as, a kipper for breakfast is enjoyed by many a piscatorial gourmet! Our smoked salmon makes an ideal filling for a sandwich or, when enjoyed as a starter for a light lunch.

Scallops, mussels and clams will help you in delivering a varied offering of seafood. Finally, I should draw your attention to government guide lines for a balanced healthy diet, details of which can be found on the internet.

Yours sincerely

Robert D Clifford-Wing
The Cornish Fishmonger

UNIT 48, WARREN ROAD, INDIAN QUEENS IND EST,
INDIAN QUEENS, CORNWALL TR9 6TL

19 Victoria Gardens
New Mills
High Peak
SK12 4BC

3rd December 2014

The Cornish Fishmonger
Unit 4, Warren Road
Indian Queens Industrial Estate
Cornwall
TR9 6TL

Dear Robert D Clifford-Wing

Thank you for your prompt and extremely informative reply to my letter of the 20th November. It enthused me enormously. So much so that I intend to start feeding fish to my three sons immediately and for seven days a week, instead of the five days I initially envisaged. You don't look a gift horse in the mouth!

In order to judge which fish are of the most benefit to the brain I will be putting my son Marcus on a diet of white fish, my middle son Henry on a diet of oily fish, and my youngest son Oscar on seafood, (mussels and cockles probably, given the exorbitant price of lobster and langoustines). After a period of time, a month should be about right I would judge, I will test as to what extent their respective diets has improved their brains, if any, and take it from there.

I am also considering feeding them kippers for breakfast every morning instead of the junk cereals they insist on dining on at the moment. Do you think the different diets idea is sound?

And the kippers?

I look forward to another of your helpful replies.

Sincerely

T Ravenscroft (Mr)

Wing OF ST MAWES THE CORNISH FISHMONGER

11th December 2014

Dear Mr Ravenscroft

Thank you for replying to my recent letter. I too am greatly enthused at the thought of your sons experiencing the scale of piscatorial excellence you so admirably make available to them around your dining table. How could one countenance looking a kipper in the mouth on a daily basis, before it disappears into one's own, is a challenge your offspring will no doubt rise to with style and panache, no doubt appropriate to their stations in life.

I feel it worth sharing my concern as to your sons' ability to ingest knowledge during their daily scholastic endeavours, as I fear excessive periods of time might be spent in the little boys room, ridding themselves of excess Omega 3 & 6 oils intent on exiting their bodies, with little concern for the classic education you so rightly seek to provide for them.

Your suggestion of specific fish diets for Marcus, Henry and Oscar meets with my guarded approval; perhaps you have a home tutor organised for Henry as, to allow him far from a sound proof WC might be a rash and ill-considered decision.

Your written word is indeed priceless as is my ability to provide you with a priced list of seafood. May I point you towards our online shop where, amongst a plethora of species, kippers are well represented?

Yours sincerely,

Robert D Clifford-Wing

UNIT 48, WARREN ROAD, INDIAN QUEENS IND EST,
INDIAN QUEENS, CORNWALL TR9 6TL

19 Victoria Gardens
New Mills
High Peak
SK12 4BC

2nd January 2014

The Cornish Fishmonger
Unit 4, Warren Road
Indian Queens Industrial Estate
Cornwall
TR9 6TL

Dear Robert D Clifford-Wing

Thank you for your continued interest and helpful advice. I can report, as you suspected might be the case, that there was an increase in Henry's bowel evacuations. Unfortunately it wasn't accompanied by an increase in his brainpower. But more of that later.

Six weeks have now passed since Oscar, Marcus and Henry were put on their respective fish diets. I made it my business to ensure that they stuck to it rigidly. The only concession I made was Christmas Dinner; however they all had kippers for breakfast that day and a prawn cocktail starter before the turkey. Yesterday I gave them an intelligence test in order to determine if their seafood regime had made any improvement to their brains, with the undermentioned results.

Prior to their commencing the diets I had set them the old brainteaser: 'A man has to transport a fox, a chicken and a bag of grain across a river in his rowing boat. Unfortunately he can only take one of them at a time. The problem is that if he takes the fox over first, the chicken, in his absence, will eat the grain. Likewise if he takes the grain over first the fox will eat the chicken. If he takes the chicken over first, followed by either the fox or the grain, either the fox will eat the chicken or the chicken will eat the grain. How does he safely transport them all to the other side?' The answer of course is that he first takes the chicken over, he comes back, takes the fox over and brings back the chicken, then takes the grain over; finally he returns and takes the chicken over. Job done.

When I had first put the problem to the boys none of them, despite much head scratching and a bribe of extra pocket money should they succeed, had the slightest idea of how to solve it. The best I got was the blankest of blank stares. Yesterday I put the problem to them again, in the hope, the ocean's bounty having been substituted for burgers, pizzas, and cornflakes in their diets, that there had been an improvement in the functioning of their grey matter. Sadly, there had not; although it must be admitted that on this occasion they did attempt answers, which might indicate the genesis of activity in their brain cells, and is something to be grateful for.

Their answers were as follows: Oscar said he would eat the chicken, it would make a change from effing fish, then take the fox over and return for the grain. Which, although the wrong answer, is an improvement on a blank stare. On hearing Oscar's answer, and no doubt learning from it - another indication of possible brain activity - Marcus said he would eat the grain, it would make a change from effing fish, then take the fox over and return for the chicken. On hearing this, and again learning from his sibling, Henry said he would eat the fox, it would make a change from effing fish, and would probably have gone on to say that he would then take the chicken across and come back for the grain, but at that point he had to excuse himself to rush to the lavatory.

On the whole a disappointing result, with just enough improvement to give hope of better things to come. The fish diets continue.

Sincerely

T Ravenscroft (Mr)

****

19 Victoria Gardens
New Mills
High Peak
SK12 4BC

17th November 2014

Iceland Foods Ltd
Second Avenue
Deeside Industrial Park
Deeside
CH5 2NW

Dear Iceland Foods

I recently returned from a two-centre holiday in Iceland. In both centres, Reykjavik and Landeyjarhofn, I was amazed to discover that there wasn't a single branch of Iceland to be found! I came across a Tesco and an Asda without any trouble, but try as I might I couldn't find so much as a trace of my favourite frozen foods store. What is the reason for this situation? I would have thought that a country called Iceland would be bursting with Icelands. I was most disappointed to say the least. I didn't want to buy anything of course - the holiday was all-inclusive - but it would have been nice to have a browse round a branch of your store in its country of origin, if only to see if they had anything on offer that they don't have in Buxton. (On reflection I might well have made a purchase, something with meat in it, preferably - after a week confined to the vagaries of the normal Icelandic diet, which seems to consist mostly of herring in various guises and disguises, my stomach was crying out for a couple of your brilliant 'Mr Brain's Pork Faggots in our Classic West Country

Sauce'.)

We plan to visit Iceland again next year. I would be looking look forward to the trip more eagerly than I am if I knew that in the meantime you had opened a few branches there. Is this possible; or just wishful thinking?

Sincerely

T Ravenscroft (Mr)

Iceland

Iceland Foods Limited
Second Avenue
Deeside Industrial Park
Flintshire
CH5 2NW

Mr T Ravenscroft
19 Victoria Gardens
New Mills
High Peak
SK12 4BC

28/11/2014

Dear Mr Ravenscroft

Thank you for your letter. Firstly, I do hope you had a great holiday to Iceland recently, and what a lovely country it is to visit.

I'm sorry you were disappointed that you could not locate an Iceland food store in Reykjavik. I have spoken with our International Stores Department who have confirmed that we have two stores in the Reykjavik area. It is disappointing that you were unable to locate one of the stores though I hope that you are able to find one when you visit Iceland again next year.

You may be interested to know that over the past 12 months we have been expanding our stores across many other European countries including Czech Republic, Republic of Ireland and many more. Our Property Department are always on the lookout for new locations so I will certainly pass a copy of your letter onto them for consideration with regards to opening more stores across Iceland.

Once again, thank you for taking the time and trouble to contact us. I hope you have another lovely holiday again next year and in the mean time, I hope to see you in your local Iceland store soon.

Kind regards

Chelsea Johnson, Iceland Customer Care

19 Victoria Gardens
New Mills
High Peak
SK12 4BC

8th December 2014

Iceland Foods Ltd
Second Avenue
Deeside Industrial Park
Deeside
CH5 2NW

Dear Chelsea

Thank you for your prompt reply. What a lovely name you have. A girl with the same name lives next door but one to me. Apparently she was named that by her mother to annoy her estranged husband, who is a Manchester United fan.

On reflection it is small wonder I didn't come across one of your shops in Iceland; it was so damned cold in Reykjavic that my glasses kept freezing over and I could barely see a yard in front of me let alone a branch of Iceland! Of course they don't tell you that in the holiday brochures. Nor do they mention the country's large dependence on reindeer meat and herrings to keep body and soul together. I'm sure I must have eaten a whole reindeer whilst over there and enough herrings to take care of my Omega oil levels for the rest of my life.

Excellent news that you hope to see me in my local Iceland Store soon. I am already looking eagerly forward to it. My nearest store is Marple, Cheshire, which I visit often. How does Tuesday the 23rd of December at 2 pm sound, or is that too near Christmas? As it will probably be very crowded at that time, what with people doing their last minute shopping, I will be wearing a red rose in my lapel for identification purposes and will position myself by the frozen vegetables.

Regarding your Property Department looking out for new locations. I may be able to help you here as my home town of New Mills would seem to fit the bill admirably. Despite a population in excess of 10,000 all that it boasts in the way of supermarkets - if boasts is the right expression - is a branch of Sainsbury's Local, with its limited stock at unlimited prices, and the Co-op, ditto. Premises wouldn't be a problem as my friend Mr Atkins assures me that he can lay hands on a 10,000 square feet warehouse that only needs a bit of work doing on the roof, and the waterwheel either removed or restored, before you could have an Iceland up and running. Ensuring that it runs efficiently would be even less of a problem as I would be available to do this personally, being at a bit of a loose end at the moment. I have no experience in retail sales, but there can't be all that much to it if the people at the Co-op can make a living at it. Perhaps we can discuss my salary and company car (a Mercedes or BMW would be nice, although I would settle for a Skoda Octavia) when we meet on the 23rd?

I look forward to hearing from you soon.

Sincerely

T Ravenscroft (Mr)

Iceland

Iceland Foods Limited
Second Avenue
Deeside Industrial Park
Flintshire
CH5 2NW

19 Victoria Gardens
New Mills
High Peak
SK12 4BC

13/12/2014

Dear Mr Ravenscroft

Thank you for writing back to us.

I don't blame you for not spotting one of the stores in Reykjavik. It is a busy city after all. It amazes me how cold it is there, I suppose walking into the Iceland Store would have been a warm welcome for you!

Unfortunately, even your local store in Marple in Cheshire is a little too far for me to travel, so I do apologise about that. Maybe you can shop in the Marple store and purchase your favourite Iceland products on 23/12/2014 as planned without me? As you stated, it will most probably be very busy on this day so I'm sure you won't notice my absence.

With regards to the new store locations, I will certainly pass on your suggestion onto our Property Department to look into. New Mills does seem to be a great location for an Iceland store after all. Maybe if we do open a store in the New Mills area you can apply for a position with us? I can assure you that working in Iceland is very rewarding. A company car may not be something we can promise, but I'm sure working with a great team would be just as favourable.

I thank you once again for taking the time to write back to us, and if I do not hear back from you soon, I hope you have a lovely Christmas.

Kind regards

Chelsea Johnson
Iceland Customer Care

19 Victoria Gardens
New Mills
High Peak
SK12 4BC

24th December 2014

Chelsea Johnson
Iceland Foods Ltd
Deeside Industrial Park
Deeside
CH5 2NW

Dear Chelsea

Sorry you weren't able to meet me as planned. In fact your letter didn't arrive until today, the 24th, by which time I had already been to your Marple branch to keep our appointment. I suspected something must have gone wrong when I had been standing by the frozen vegetables for the best part of an hour and no one had spoken to me apart from a woman who accused me of 'lurking'. So after I'd done a bit of shopping I threw in the towel and went home. I gave the red rose to the checkout girl with the squint and wished her a Merry Christmas. She was quite charmed by this and didn't charge me for my Heinz Spaghetti Hoops, although that may have been an error.

Great news that you will be opening a branch of Iceland in New Mills. I am already looking forward to shopping in it. My friend Mr Atkins asked me to remind you that the roof will need repairing prior to your moving in, but he knows a man.

Sincerely

T Ravenscroft (Mr)

****

19 Victoria Gardens
New Mills
High Peak
SK12 4BC

26th November 2014

Innocent
Fruit Towers
342 Ladbroke Grove
London
W10 5BU

Dear Innocent

My wife, my three children and I all drink from your range of fruit drinks, and very nice they are too. I've tried them all, but if pushed I would have to say that my favourite thirst quencher is the apple, whilst my wife loves nothing better than getting a big bottle of tropical juice inside her. The kids don't have favourites - they love them all!

Naturally the children always consume the drinks neat - and usually straight from the bottle, whereas my wife and I always use a glass - but occasionally I add a small measure of whisky or brandy to mine. Well a bit more than occasionally, and a bit more than a small measure, if I am to be entirely truthful. My wife adds gin. I can't say that the addition of alcohol improves the taste of your drinks because that would be telling a lie - however it does have the effect of mellowing my mood considerably, especially when I've had a couple.

Bearing this in mind, have you ever thought of introducing an alcoholic version of your excellent product? You could perhaps call it 'Innocent - But Just a Touch Guilty'. I'm sure you would have a winner.

Sincerely

T Ravenscroft (Mr)

innocent

7th December 2014

Dear Mr Ravenscroft

We're chuffed to hear that you're such a big fan of our drinks - while we're all about natural, healthy drinks (which means no alcohol we're afraid) I've included our festive cocktail recipes. Feel free to make your own additions (if you know what we mean)!

Anne Brownhill

Customer Services, Innocent.

**innocent drinks, Fruit Towers, 342 Ladbroke Grove, London, W10 5BU**

19 Victoria Gardens
New Mills
High Peak
SK12 4BC

11th December 2014

Anne Brownhill
Innocent
Fruit Towers
342 Ladbroke Grove
London
W10 5BU

Dear Anne

Thank you for the ten poundsworth of vouchers and the festive cocktail recipes.

The following day we spent the vouchers on a range of your drinks, and the same evening used them to try the range of cocktails. I can report a great success story. At our age - 'middle' - we aren't as active in the bed department as I would like us to be, but after drinking our way from 'A Pomegranate in a Pink Apple Tree' through 'Three Merry Berries and Five Gold Things' to 'Six Spices Muddling', all generously laced with alcohol, my wife couldn't get me into our bedroom fast enough, and it wasn't even Saturday night. The following evening we worked our way from 'Seven Sips a Sparkling' to 'Twelve Cinnamon Drummers Drumming' with the same blissful outcome. I don't know whether they have made me any healthier but they've certainly made me a lot happier!

We hope to drink many more 'Sinnocents' (my name for your cocktails, please feel free to use it) in the future. I really do think you should market them, perhaps with the slogan - both with a nod toward their health-giving properties, and to paraphrase Shakespeare - ‘Stimulates the desire and enhances the performance’.

Sincerely

T Ravenscroft (Mr)

****

19 Victoria Gardens
New Mills
High Peak
SK12 4BC

24th November 2014

Kingsmill Careline
Vanwall Road
Maidenhead
SL6 4UF

Dear Kingsmill

I thought the time long overdue before I wrote to you in praise of your white sliced bread. It certainly beats the bread of your competitors, and I've tried them all. Kingsmill bread is soft, white, and although not too thick is substantial enough to hold its chosen filling adequately, which is the main requirement of a slice of bread. When you add to this the fact that Kingsmill is a bread without any discernible taste, thus ensuring that it doesn't interfere with the flavour of your chosen filling, you are in bread heaven. After all, it is the filling that is of interest to the consumer of the sandwich, not the bread: Lord Sandwich, who the sandwich is named after, as I'm sure you will be well aware, was not interested in the bread when he asked his servants to bring him slivers of meat between two slices of bread to the gaming tables; it was the meat inside that was the attraction.

The only fault I can find with your bread, and it is a very small fault, is that it is perhaps a little *too* soft, and because of this often attaches itself to the roof of my dentures when I'm chewing it, especially with softer fillings such as tuna mayonnaise and cream cheese (it isn't as bad with sliced meat and cheese, although it does still tend to cling on a bit.) When this happens I have to poke it free with my index finger, which is a bit of a nuisance, if not inelegant, especially when eating out, but is a small price to pay for a bread so absolutely tasteless that it never detracts from the enjoyment of the filling by a single iota. However, should you know of a way I can prevent this happening, it would be greatly appreciated it if you could pass it on to me.

Finally, when are we going to see the delightful Mel and Sue advertising your white sliced loaves once again? Or can't you afford them now that they're presenting the hit *Great British Bake Off* show on TV? If their fee has gone up because of this I would gladly pay another penny per loaf for the chance to be entertained by them again, as I'm sure all your customers would.

Sincerely

T Ravenscroft (Mr)

**CONSUMER SERVICES**
**Kingsmill place**
**Vanwall Road**
**Maidenhead**
**SL6 4UF**

Ref: 4404496

01/12/2014

Mr Ravenscroft
19 Victoria Gardens
New Mills
High Peak
SK12 4BC

Dear Mr Ravenscroft

Thank you very much for taking the trouble to write with your comments about our Kingsmill Soft White bread that we bake.

We were pleased to hear you enjoy using our bread to make your sandwiches. I have passed your letter on to our Marketing Department, as I know how much they value customers opinions.

Pleased find enclosed voucher to the value of £1.00 which we would like you to accept to go towards your next purchase.

Yours sincerely,

Jodie Miller
Consumer Service Advisor.

19 Victoria Gardens
New Mills
High Peak
SK12 4BC

5th December 2014

Jodie Miller
Kingsmill Careline
Vanwall Road
Maidenhead
SL6 4UF

Your ref: Ref: 4404496

Dear Jodie

Thank you for your letter and the voucher for £1. Every little helps, as Tesco are fond of telling us. (Although it doesn't appear to be helping them very much at the moment, by all accounts.)

Apparently you don't know of anything that might stop your bread clinging to the roof of one's mouth with as much resolve as Leo DiCaprio clung on to the lifeboat in *Titanic,* or no doubt you would have offered advice on how to stop this happening; but not to worry, since writing to you I have discovered that Roberts's white sliced doesn't do this at all, and is almost as good as Kingsmill, so I've changed to Roberts until such time as you can sort out this problem.

Now a word of warning. In my first letter you will recall that I expressed a hope that we might see Mel and Sue back on our TV screens advertising your bread. Unfortunately I have since learned that Sue is a lesbian. Now it isn't for me to tell a woman how to behave, nor would I, and I am just about the least homophobic man you could hope to meet; however, having said that, I sincerely hope you will now abandon any plans you may have had of employing Sue again. I mean for all you know, prior to shooting the commercial she might have been involved in whatever lesbians get up to behind closed doors, and, having been involved in it....well you wouldn't want her getting her hands in your dough, would you? Just thought I'd mention it, a word to the wise and all that.

I am thinking of putting the £1 voucher towards a packet of Oatilicious. Is this product suitable for vegans?

Sincerely

T Ravenscroft (Mr)

**CONSUMER SERVICES**
**Kingsmill place**
**Vanwall Road**
**Maidenhead**
**SL6 4UF**

Ref: 4404496

09/12/2014

Mr T Ravenscroft
19 Victoria Gardens
New Mills

Dear Mr Ravenscroft

We are writing to you in connection with your letter dated 5th December.

Our bread is designed to be a soft bread and we are sorry if you find this clings to the roof of your mouth.

We are glad to hear you are going to use the voucher. The Kingsmill Oatilcious bread is in fact suitable for vegans and we hope you enjoy it.

Yours sincerely,

Jodie Miller
Consumer Service Advisor

19 Victoria Gardens
New Mills
High Peak
SK12 4BC

11th December 2014

Jodie Miller
Kingsmill Careline
Vanwall Road
Maidenhead
SL6 4UF

Your ref: Ref: 4404496

Dear Jodie

Great news! Not only is your Oatilicious bread suitable for vegans but it doesn't cling to the roof of your mouth when you chew it! If you could now guarantee that you will prevent Sue Perkins from getting anywhere near it I will be a happy man.

Sincerely

T Ravenscroft (Mr)

****

19 Victoria Gardens
New Mills
High Peak
SK12 4BC

28th December 2014

Bannisters' Farm
Farmhouse Potato Bakers Limited
Lancaster Road
Bridlington

YO15 3QY

Dear Bannisters' Farm

An enthusiastic epicure of long-standing, always on the lookout for something unusual to tempt my palate, I was pleased to come across your website whilst recently surfing the internet in search of a new culinary experience. I refer of course to your 'Fully Loaded Jackets, absolutely jam-packed with five delicious fillings'. Well I am a man who loves his jam so wasting no time at all I bought one each of your 'Cheese & Beans' and 'Chicken & Mushroom'.

I have to say I was disappointed. There was no jam in them! They were fully loaded with cheese & beans and chicken & mushrooms, you will find no argument from me there; however they were not fully loaded, or even partially loaded, with jam.

In fact both the Cheese & Beans and Chicken & Mushroom jacket potatoes were quite tasty and a credit to you, and I may well buy more, but that's hardly the point is it?

I have just one question. Why trick people into thinking there is jam in your Fully Loaded Jackets if there isn't?

Sincerely

T Ravenscroft (Mr)

BANNISTERS' FARM

Mr T Ravenscroft
19 Victoria Gardens
New Mills
High Peak
SK12 4BC

15 January 2015

Dear Mr Ravenscroft

**Bannisters' Farm Fully Loaded Jacket Potatoes**

Thank you very much for your letter dated 28 December 2014 which we were both interested and perplexed to read. We are sincerely sorry to learn of your disappointment relating to the absence of jam in our Fully Loaded Jacket Potatoes.

In our, perhaps over-zealous, attempt to emphasise the extreme loadedness of our Fully Loaded Jackets on our website, it appears we have inadvertently created an expectation of sweetness in our jackets.

Please be assured this was not our intention and whilst we are delighted that you enjoyed our product despite the lack of fruit preserves, we would like to offer you the enclosed pot of jam, to be added separately if required, to your future purchases.

Since, as you rightly point out, our current products do not contain jam as an ingredient, we have also passed on your suggestion for perusal by my colleague who deals with out "New Product Development" - we are always open to suggestions!

Once again, we apologise for your disappointment and we hope you continue to buy our jam-free products.

Yours sincerely,

Zoe Bannister.

**Lancaster Road, Carnaby Industrial Estate,**
**Bridlington, YO15 3QY**

19 Victoria Gardens
New Mills
High Peak
SK12 4BC

20th January 2015

Bannisters' Farm
Farmhouse Potato Bakers Limited
Lancaster Road
Bridlington
YO15 3QY

Dear Zoe Bannister

Thank you for the strawberry jam. What a lovely and generous thought. My wife had a spoonful of it on her breakfast crumpet and I had the remainder on one of your Broccoli and Cauliflower Cheese Jackets. A dish to die for. In fact our cat almost did die, when I put my leavings down for it, and for reasons not readily apparent, choked on it.

Your colleague who deals with "New Product Development" could do worse than add it to your range of jacket potatoes; he certainly doesn't seem to have stretched himself in creating your current, rather prosaic choices. To help redress this, might I also suggest a 'Cornish Fishmonger Home Smoked Kipper Jacket, and a Dairylea Dunker Jacket? Jam-packed of course.

Sincerely

T Ravenscroft (Mr)

****

19 Victoria Gardens
New Mills
High Peak
SK12 4BC

24th February 2015

Young's Seafood Limited
Ross House
Wickham Road
Grimsby
DN31 3SW

Dear Young's

At the moment I have my three sons on a fish diet, in a controlled effort to improve their brains. To this end the splendid Robert D Clifford-Wing of The Cornish Fish Merchant has helped me compile a suitable diet for them. Of my sons, Marcus is on a diet of white fish - cod, haddock etc, whilst Oscar is on a seafood diet, - crab, prawns etc.

Ever anxious to make their diets as varied as possible - within the confines mentioned above - I picked up a packet of your Seafood Sticks, with the intention of feeding them to Oscar to see how he got on with them. On opening the packet I paused to read the list of ingredients, whereupon I was surprised to find that there was no mention of prawns, nor of crab, nor of shrimps, in fact no reference at all to any foods generally regarded as seafood. There was however, a mention of Surimi, an unknown substance to me, and Pollock, a white fish with which I - along with Marcus, now - am familiar.

If it isn't too much trouble, could you please

explain to me why something labelled seafood contains nothing recognisable as seafood in it?

Sincerely

T Ravenscroft (Mr)

Young's
SEAFOOD LIMITED

20/03/2015

Mr T Ravenscroft
19 Victoria Gardens
New Mills
High Peak
SK12 4BC

Dear Mr Ravenscroft

Thank you for contacting us regarding our Young's Seafood Sticks.

The surimi contained in this product is based on an ancient Japanese delicacy. Today's surimi products are made in modern factories using techniques to create the distinctive white, flaky material. Surimi or seafood sticks are not made directly from fish fillets, but from pure protein which is extracted from the meat by washing processes.

Surimi is very convenient and versatile. It is ready to eat and requires no cooking. Guaranteed to be boneless, Surimi is great for children.

I can confirm that our Seafood Sticks contain 35% surimi of which 91.5% is fish protein from Alaskan Pollock. The product is made by combining this Surimi with other ingredients to help add texture, flavour and colour. Crustacean flavouring is used and hence there is the required allergy advice printed on the pack.

I would like to take this opportunity t o reassure you that every possible care is taken in the formulation, and manufacture and distribution of all our products to ensure that they meet the customer's requirements. As a responsible Company we frequently seek guidance from Trading Standards and other regulating bodies to ensure our packaging and product fully complies with all the appropriate legislation. In addition to this all products are consumer tested prior to launch.

I trust that you will accept, without prejudice, the enclosed Voucher to the value of £2.50 as a gesture of our goodwill and that you will continue to enjoy purchases from our range of products in the future.

Yours sincerely

Roy Backrath
Customer Care Co-ordinator.

**Consumer Care Dept, Ross House, Wickham Rd, Grimsby, DN31 3SW**

19 Victoria Gardens
New Mills
High Peak
SK12 4BC

23rd March 2015

Roy Backrath
Young's Seafood Limited
Ross House
Wickham Road
Grimsby
DN31 3SW

Dear Roy Backrath

Thank you for your reply explaining the make-up of your Seafood Sticks. It did everything but tell me why, given that there is nothing in them that is generally regarded as seafood, you choose to call them Seafood Sticks. It can't be because you are trying to fool people into thinking they are something they are not, as I am quite sure that a reputable company such as Young's would never adopt such disingenuous tactics. So why is it?

Sincerely

T Ravenscroft (Mr)

NO REPLY!

****

19 Victoria Gardens
New Mills
High Peak
SK12 4BC

11th February 2015

The Big Bean Company
Highfields Business Park
Leeds
HX6 8DB

Dear Big Bean Company

Some weeks ago I chanced upon an article on the internet that recommended the implementation of a correct diet as something that might help to combat the effects of impotence. The article quoted actual cases along with testimonials that spoke of the efficaciousness of a judicious food intake, along with advice on avoiding artery-clogging trans-fats. One of the things it strongly advocated was the consumption of more vegetable protein; it particularly recommended beans, especially beans that are familiarly known as 'baked beans'. I must say I was a bit dubious about this claim as a plate of baked beans, often accompanied by bacon, is invariably the staple diet of cowboys in Western films, and I don't recall John Wayne getting his legover all that often if you discount him getting on his horse. However...

I am not a man to take half measures so took no time in putting myself on a diet that included a generous portion of your Big Baked Beans as part of each meal; breakfast, lunch, dinner and supper. Happily I can report that after not much more than a month I am already experiencing a big improvement 'down there'.

I don't know if you at The Big Bean Company are aware of this additional benefit contained in its baked beans, or not, but in my opinion it isn't a thing that should be kept secret. In fact I think it would be a crying shame if you didn't make it better known to the general public, as you could be doing a lot of men a big favour.

I would be interested to know if any of your other customers have derived similar benefits.

Sincerely

T Ravenscroft (Mr)

**The Big Bean Company**

19 Victoria Gardens
New Mills
High Peak
SK12 4BC

18th February 2015
Our Ref: 245972/RA

Dear Mr Ravenscroft

Thank you for your letter of the 11th inst. It is always nice to hear from a satisfied customer, especially one who is especially satisfied with our beans!

In fact we have heard of this sort of thing before. Unfortunately we are unable to mention it in our advertising, or display it on our cans, as it may not work as well for some people, or even at all, and we wouldn't want to disappoint anyone (or be sued by them if they failed to get the right results!).

I enclose a voucher to the value of £5 so you can enjoy more of our Big Baked Beans, and as an aid to your revitalized sex life.

Yours Sincerely,

Joan Johnson.
Customer Relations.

**THE BIG BEAN CO, HIGHFIELDS BUSINESS PARK, LEEDS, HX6 8DB**

19 Victoria Gardens
New Mills
High Peak
SK12 4BC

22nd February 2015

Joan Johnson
The Big Bean Company
Highfields Business Park
Leeds
HX6 8DB

Dear Joan Johnson

Further to my letter of the 11th Feb and your gracious reply I must report that I have hit something of a snag. Your beans are working as well as ever and have completely cured the erectile dysfunction problem I was experiencing. However, most disappointingly, it hasn't led to my having sex with my wife again on a regular basis. This is because although my diet of Big Baked Beans has made me fit for purpose in the bedroom it has also made me very flatulent; so flatulent in fact that my wife won't allow me in the bedroom. We did manage to have sex once, in the open air, (the local park) but it was far from satisfactory as halfway through it started raining and we were wet through by the time we'd finished. (And we were *always* going to finish!)

With the above in mind, can you recommend anything I can take that might combat

the flatulence enhancing property of your baked

beans, whilst at the same time maintaining their erectile capabilities.

Sincerely

T Ravenscroft (Mr)

**The Big Bean Company**

19 Victoria Gardens
New Mills
High Peak
SK12 4BC

8th February 2015

Our Ref: 245972/RA

Dear Mr Ravenscroft

Happily, I can help you! My mother - also a big fan of our beans - used to suffer from flatulence, so I am in a position to pass on good advice about this complaint. My mum's remedy is to eat 2 to 3 small tubs of bio-yogurt a day. She also takes half-a-dozen ginger capsules a day (or eats a fresh chunk of ginger, about two square inches). The only other thing she does, on the few occasions the bio-yogurt and ginger have failed to have the desired effect, is to kneel on her bed with her head down and her bottom in the air, a position that allows any wind to escape more easily.

I hope this is helpful and good luck!

Yours Sincerely,

Joan Johnson.
Customer Relations.

**THE BIG BEAN CO, HIGHFIELDS BUSINESS PARK, LEEDS, HX6 8DB**

19 Victoria Gardens
New Mills
High Peak
SK12 4BC

2nd March 2015

Joan Johnson
The Big Bean Company
Highfields Business Park
Leeds
HX6 8DB

Dear Joan Johnson

I am trying your recommendation of 2 to 3 small tubs of bio-yogurt and ginger, but there has been no change for the good as yet. It is early days though, and I shall persist. I will not, however, unlike your mother, be kneeling on the bed with my head down and my bottom in the air, even if it does allow the wind to escape more easily; I suffer with my back enough as it is. However it does suggest an interesting position that my wife might adopt if ever she lets me back in the bedroom, so here's hoping.

Sincerely

T Ravenscroft (Mr)

****

19 Victoria Gardens
New Mills
High Peak
SK12 4BC

6th January 2015

Highland Spring Group
Stirling Street
Blackford
Perthshire
PH4 1QA

Dear Highland Spring

For some time I have been a consumer of both your Highland Spring mineral water and your more upmarket Speyside Glenlivet water, and have never had cause for complaint, indeed far from it. However something transpired recently to which I feel I must draw your attention, as in all probability you will wish to take steps to ensure that it doesn't happen again. The details are:-

At a travelling fair my middle son Henry won a goldfish, which he brought home in a plastic bag provided for that very purpose. As we don't have a goldfish bowl, and until such time as we could purchase one, I temporarily billeted the goldfish in a large cut glass flower vase that wasn't in use at the time. From my own childhood I recalled that a long and happy life is rarely the fate of goldfishes won at travelling fairs, and with this in mind thought I would give the little fellow every chance of survival by filling the vase with Speyside Glenlivet in preference to tap water. The following morning it was stone dead!

It could of course have been that the vase, being long and thin as opposed to a goldfish bowl being squat and wide, presented an environment that the goldfish was uncomfortable with; however I recall that as a child I once kept a goldfish in a wellington boot for three weeks, so this seems unlikely.

That led me into thinking that it is more than likely it was your mineral water that was the problem. In your advertising literature you make great claims regarding the purity of your Speyside Glenlivet - and I am sure you do not exaggerate its wholesomeness - but at the same time you also contend that it has an unusually low mineral content; so perhaps it is the paucity of minerals in it that did for the goldfish?

I would appreciate your comments.

Sincerely

T Ravenscroft (Mr)

Mr T Ravenscroft
19 Victoria Gardens
New Mills
High Peak
SK12 4BC

09/01/2015

Dear Mr Ravenscroft

**RE - customer complaint regarding Speyside Glenlivet Mineral Water**

We are very sorry to learn of the death of the goldfish your son won at the fair. I can completely understand this is an extremely upsetting situation for your son, especially after the excitement of winning the fish in the first place.

Unfortunately we cannot give an answer as to how this may have occurred, however the following may be a contributing factor. Goldfish need oxygen in water to survive, and natural ground water has naturally low levels of dissolved oxygen. Therefore once the present oxygen has been used up, it is depleted, and needs to be replenished in the form of a pump or something similar.

I hope this has answered your query.

Sincerely,

Kymberley Munro
Group Technical Assistant
Highland Spring Group

**HIGHLAND SPRING LIMITED**
**Stirling Street, Blackford, Perthshire PH4 1QA**

19 Victoria Gardens
New Mills
High Peak
SK12 4BC

12th January 2015

Kymberley Munro
Highland Spring Group
Stirling Street
Blackford
Perthshire
PH4 1QA

Dear Kymberley

Thank you for your prompt reply to my letter.

Unfortunately I inadvertently misled you. What actually happened was that when my wife presented me with the problem of where to accommodate the goldfish I said: 'We'll give it the best chance of survival, fill the vase with Glenlivet'. Apparently she misunderstood me and used not Glenlivet Mineral Water, as I meant, but a couple of bottles of my Glenlivet Single Malt whisky. We must assume that the goldfish died very quickly, but very happy.

Fortunately when I fished the goldfish out it didn't appear to have done the whisky any harm - which can't of course be said for the effect the whisky had on the goldfish - and it is still in a fit state to drink (half and half with your excellent Glenlivet Mineral Water, as is my preference). Nor was the goldfish wasted, as all three of my sons are on a fish diet at the moment, so Henry (the goldfish's owner, you will recall) was able to eat it. He said it was very nice, better than his usual mackerel or herring. I can well understand that it was - I wouldn't have turned my nose up at Glenlivet marinated goldfish myself!

Sincerely

T Ravenscroft (Mr)

****

19 Victoria Gardens
New Mills
High Peak
SK12 4BC

29th January 2015

Her Majesty the Queen
Buckingham Palace
London
SW1A 1AA

Dear Your Majesty

I was surfing the net this morning on the lookout for a supply of cheap fish - my three sons are on a fish diet and obviously, that commodity being the price it is, the cheaper I can obtain it the better - when I chanced upon a news article, the content of which might be to our mutual advantage. The item informed me that any sturgeon caught in British waters automatically becomes the property of the reigning monarch, but that notwithstanding this the Queen usually waived her rights and allowed any fisherman catching a sturgeon to keep it for himself. The article quoted the case of a fisherman in Swansea who benefited from Your Maj's largesse, mentioning that the fish, a ten feet long, 300 pound specimen, was sold to a London restaurant for £27 per pound.

I am aware that despite your well-documented and deserved reputation for thriftiness that you get a bit strapped at times, and have difficulty making ends meet. With this in mind might I suggest that in future, instead of telling the catcher of a sturgeon that he can keep the fish, you sell it to me? I would be willing to pay you £10 per pound and would stand the delivery charge, or pick it up myself if it hasn't been landed too far from my address. This would really help me out with my sons' diet, fishwise.

I hope to hear from you soon with a positive reply.

Sincerely

T Ravenscroft (Mr)

**BUCKINGHAM PALACE**

23RD February 2015

Dear Mr Ravenscroft

Thank you for your note of 29th January addressed to The Queen from which careful note has been taken of your comments.

Perhaps I may refer you in the first instance to the website of the Department for the Environment, Food and Rural Affairs, under the section concerning sturgeon. Although the offence and protections listed there are for the common sturgeon, unless stated, all species of sturgeon are also protected by the Convention of Trade in Endangered Species of Fauna and Flora (CITES).

I hope this information is helpful to you.

Yours sincerely,

Miss Jennie Vine
Deputy Correspondence Coordinator.

****

19 Victoria Gardens
New Mills
High Peak
SK12 4BC

25th November 2014

Dairylea
Cadbury House
Sanderson Road
Uxbridge
UB8 1DH

Dear Dairylea

I'm afraid I have a complaint about your Dairylea Dunkers. On dunking them in my tea they always dissolve more or less immediately and collapse into the cup. On only very rare occasions have I managed to get them out in one piece, but never in such a solid state that they haven't fallen back into the tea, or worse still on the tablecloth, before I have managed to transport them the short distance to my mouth. They really don't give you a sporting chance; and there nothing wrong with my reflexes believe me, I can still catch a fly in mid air.

I suppose I have been spoiled with HobNobs and ginger biscuits, both of which you can dunk in your tea and leave safely for a few seconds with impunity and without their collapsing. You can't leave your Dairylea Dunkers in for a split second, never mind a few! This is a great shame because I've tried them without dunking and they are quite tasty. But if you eat them without dunking they can't rightly aspire to the name Dunkers, can they?

There's also the matter of the cheese that comes along with them. Why is this? If I'd wanted cheese I would have bought some. In my opinion your Dunkers are a perfectly acceptable biscuit in their own right, without your having to give free cheese with them, in what can only be seen as an effort to bribe people into buying them. In my opinion you would be far better off spending the money you waste on free cheese in adding something to your recipe to make them a little less pliable when coming into contact with hot tea.

It is all quite depressing.

Sincerely

T Ravenscroft (Mr)

Mondelēz International

Mr T Ravenscroft
19 Victoria Gardens
New Mills
High Peak
SK12 4BC

03 December 2014

Dear Mr Ravenscroft

Thank you for contacting us concerning Dairylea Dunkers.

About you idea for a new Dairylea biscuit! Let me take this opportunity to say that Mondelez UK receives a large number of suggestions from consumers and entrepreneurs, but in order to avoid misunderstandings over ownership rights, we are unable to accept any ideas from outside the company's pre-contracted resources.

Dairylea have many development ideas every year but what you are suggesting will not be one we will work on.

Please understand that these precautions are for the benefit of all parties and that this is not a judgement on the quality of your idea, however you are taking the biscuit by saying you use them to dunk into your hot cup of tea.

Dairylea Dunkers are an absolute favourite with little kids, big kids and the kid in you. Take one stick. And dunk it into that dairylicious cheese.

Thank you for considering Dairylea.

Kind regards,

Eoin Kelly
Consumer Relations Team.

**Cadbury House Uxbridge Business Park Sanderson Road Uxbridge UB8 1DH**

*

19 Victoria Gardens
New Mills
High Peak
SK12 4BC

10th December 2014

Eoin Kelly
Mondelez UK Ltd
Cadbury House
Sanderson Road
Uxbridge
UB8 1DH

Dear Eoin Kelly

I don't know about me 'taking the biscuit', as you put it, but I certainly think you are taking the mickey with your suggestion that I should 'Take one stick. And dunk it right into that dairylicious cheese.'

I tried this, and although I am prepared to concede that coated in 'dairylicious' cheese the stick takes a bit longer to melt, it still does not take long enough to enable me to take it out of the tea before it disintegrates and falls into the cup. Not only does this render it inedible but it exacerbates the problem by depositing the cheese in the tea, rendering it totally undrinkable.

Maybe it is time for you to have a re-think about your policy of not accepting ideas and suggestions from outside your company's pre-constructed sources. Either that or get your pre-constructed sources to get their fingers out!

Sincerely

T Ravenscroft (Mr)

## NO REPLY!

****

19 Victoria Gardens
New Mills
High Peak
SK12 4BC

26th November 2014

Lidl Ltd
19 Worple Road
Wimbledon
London
SW19 4JS

Dear Lidl

There has been much in the newspapers and on TV lately about the Lidl and Aldi supermarkets and their effect on their British counterparts. That being the case I thought I'd get myself along to my nearest branch of Lidl to see what all the fuss is about. What a revelation! I usually do my groceries shopping at Tesco and Iceland, occasionally Morrisons, and, when I'm absolutely desperate and nowhere else is open, the Co-op. Suffice to say that in future I will be giving my business to these stores much less readily; for not only did I find that the prices at Lidl, for the same quality of goods, were on average about 30% less expensive, but also that the range of products to be had there, whilst maybe not as extensive as that of Tesco and the others, was extensive enough for all but the most choosy of shoppers.

Whilst I was surprised at this I was even more surprised to learn that your company is German. I say surprised because I spent a holiday in Germany a couple of years ago and the only things they seem to eat over there eat are pork and potatoes, and in unhealthy quantities at that.

Maybe those comestibles are all you have left over there after you've filled up all your shops over here? One thing is for certain - we may well have beaten you soundly in two World Wars but you can certainly master us when it comes to flogging groceries. Perhaps Hitler would have been better off invading us with merchandisers rather than Messerschmitts and Doodlebugs? So much for Napoleon referring to the British as a nation of shopkeepers!

Anyway, good luck to you, keep it up, and *auf wiedersehen* as you say in Germany, from a very satisfied customer. And please keep me notified of any special offers you have coming up in future.

Sincerely

T Ravenscroft (Mr)

Without Prejudice

**Lidl UK GmbH**
**Tailend Farm**
**Deans Road**
**Livingston**
**EH54 8SE**

Mr T Ravenscroft
19 Victory Gardens
High Peak
SK22 4LL

03-Dec-2014
Our Ref: #9936919 CS

Dear Mr Ravenscroft

**Re: Stock Range**

Thank you for taking the time to contact us.

We take great pride in selling high quality products at competitive prices and providing a pleasant shopping experience for all our customers. Comments and suggestions from our customers help us to maintain the high standards we aim for.

Your comments have been brought to the attention of the relevant department.

We hope you will remain a valued customer.

Hollie Brown
**Customer Service**

19 Victoria Gardens
New Mills
High Peak
SK12 4BC

16th December 2014

Hollie Brown
Lidl Ltd
19 Worple Road
Wimbledon
London
SW19 4JS

Dear Hollie Brown

I hope one of the relevant departments you bring the attention of my letter to is the department responsible for mailing letters, since they got my address wrong, with the result that the letter took almost two weeks to arrive, having been redirected.

Despite what I said in my original letter I will not be shopping with you again as there has been a serious development.

Sincerely

T Ravenscroft (Mr)

Without Prejudice

**Lidl UK GmbH**
**Tailend Farm**
**Deans Road**
**Livingston**
**EH54 8SE**

Mr T Ravenscroft
19 Victoria Gardens
New Mills
High Peak
SK12 4BC

14-Jan-2015
Our Ref: #9936919

Dear Mr Ravenscroft

**Re: Lidl Store: Manchester Road MANCHESTER**

Thank you for taking the time to contact me again regarding the above mentioned store.

In order for me to look into the matter, I require some additional information, please provide further details of the serious development you refer to in your letter.

I look forward to your reply.

Emma Cohen
**Customer Service**

19 Victoria Gardens
New Mills
High Peak
SK12 4BC

10th January 2015

Lidl UK GmbH
Tailend Farm
Deans Road
Livingston
EH54 8SE

Your Ref: #9936919

Dear Emma Cohen

**Re: The Serious Development**

You will no doubt find out in due course.

Sincerely

T Ravenscroft (Mr)

****

19 Victoria Gardens
New Mills
High Peak
SK12 4BC

3rd January 2015

The Rt Hon David Cameron MP
10 Downing Street
London
SW1A 2AA

Dear Prime Minister

I reproduce below an extract from a letter I recently sent to the German supermarket chain LIDL

*There has been much in the newspapers and on TV lately about Lidl and Aldi and their effect on the traditional British supermarkets so I thought I'd get along to my nearest branch of Lidl to see what all the fuss is about. What a revelation! I usually do my groceries shopping at Tesco and Iceland, occasionally Morrisons, and, when I'm absolutely desperate and nowhere else is open, the Co-op. Suffice to say that in future I will be giving my business to these stores much less readily; for not only did I find that the prices at Lidl, for the same quality of goods, were on average about 30% less expensive, but also that the range of products to be had there, whilst maybe not as extensive as that of Tesco and the others, was extensive enough for all but the most choosy of shoppers.*

*Whilst I was surprised at this I was even more surprised to learn that your company is German. I say surprised because I spent a holiday in*

*Germany a couple of years ago and the only things they seemed to eat there were pork and potatoes, and in unhealthy quantities at that. Maybe those comestibles are all you have left over there after you've filled up all your shops over here? One thing is for certain - we may well have beaten you soundly in two World Wars but you can certainly master us when it comes to flogging groceries. Perhaps Hitler would have been better off invading us with merchandisers rather than Messerschmitts and Doodlebugs? So much for Napoleon referring to the British as a nation of shopkeepers!*

Reflecting on my letter the other day it suddenly dawned on me what is happening under our very noses; the Germans, having failed to conquer our country by military means, have set about becoming our masters by controlling our food supplies! Already they have made a massive impact; the decreasing profits at Tesco and Morrisons attest to this. It can't be very long before Asda and Sainsbury's follow them, if I know anything about German ruthlessness.

It is quite obvious the way things are likely to go. Vast numbers of our population will soon begin to starve, followed by even vaster numbers when their savings run out. Probably - I wouldn't put it past them, as history tells us that Germans are capable of anything - Lidl and Aldi, backed by their Teutonic masters, will then make food available at the old prices, *but only to holders of a German passport, which will be freely available to all on relinquishing their British Citizenship.* Facing starvation people will rush to avail themselves of the said German passport. Very soon we will all be Germans. And the German government will have achieved their aim; to finally conquer Great Britain!

I really think something should be done about this. And who better to instigate it than you, Prime Minister?

I enclose £1 for your party funds, a token gesture I know, but all I can afford at the moment, thanks to the current economic climate inflicted on us by the previous Socialist government.

Sincerely

T Ravenscroft (Mr)

**10 DOWNING STREET**
LONDON SW1A 2AA

From The Direct Communications Unit

20th January 2015

Mr T Ravenscroft
19 Victoria Gardens
New Mills
High Peak
SK12 4BC

Dear Mr Ravenscroft

I am writing on behalf of the Prime Minister to thank you for your letter of 3 January. The money mentioned in your correspondence, was regrettably not enclosed.

Mr Cameron very much appreciates you taking the time and trouble to inform him of your views.

With best wishes.

Yours sincerely

C Scott
Correspondence Officer.

19 Victoria Gardens
New Mills
High Peak
SK12 4BC

The Rt Hon David Cameron MP
10 Downing Street
London
SW1A 2AA

Dear Prime Minister

I regret to inform you that you have a thief in 10 Downing Street.

I wrote to you on 3rd January expressing my concerns regarding German-owned British supermarkets. You are no doubt by now hard at work eradicating the problem. (A tip - on no account get Lord Sugar to assist you, the man is a rogue.)

Along with the letter I enclosed £1 for your party funds. On the 20th January a C Scott from your Direct Communications Unit replied to my letter, saying that the £1 was not enclosed. This is a blatant lie. The man obviously pocketed it himself. Are you sure he isn't a covert member of UKIP?

I enclose another £1 in the hope that this time it finds its way to you. But I wouldn't hold my breath if I were you.

Sincerely

T Ravenscroft (Mr)

****

19 Victoria Gardens
New Mills
High Peak
SK12 4BC

16th December 2014

Nestlé Consumer Service
P0 Box 203
York
YO1 1XY

Dear Nestle

Could you please help to settle a £50 bet I have with my wife? It concerns the pronunciation of the name Nestlé. I say it is pronounced 'Nessel' but know-it-all insists it is pronounced 'Nestlay'. You may at the same time be able to help me with another matter. I have never been a great lover of chocolate. However, following the end of a meal in a Chinese restaurant in London recently, the waiter gave me a wafer-thin, square, mint-flavoured chocolate, which on tasting I found to be quite delicious. In order that I could buy some later I asked the waiter for the name of the chocolate. He said they were called 'Affreyeymin'. Since then I have tried to buy Affreyeymin in every sweet shop in my locality. However no one seems to have heard of them, except perhaps for the woman at Thornton's, who for reasons best known to herself was quite abusive.

It occurred to me that Affreyeymin could perhaps be Chinese in origin, specially imported from China by the restaurant. However it could also be that Affreyeymin aren't very popular in this part of the country and as such are unobtainable. With this in mind I am writing to all the main chocolate manufacturers to ask them if they make Affreyeymin, and if so who is my nearest supplier. I hope you can help me.

Sincerely

T Ravenscroft (Mr)

**Nestlé Consumer Service**
**P0 Box 203**
**York**
**YO1 1XY**

22nd December 2014

Mr T Ravenscroft
19 Victoria Gardens
New Mills
High Peak
SK12 4BC

OUR REF 97260387

Dear Mr Ravenscroft

Thank you for your recent letter requesting a supply of Quality Street advertising material.

In answer to your question I can tell you that your wife is correct & that the name of our company is pronounced as 'nestlay'.

Thank you once again for taking the trouble to contact us and for the interest you have shown in our Company.

Yours sincerely

V Severs (Miss)
Administration Officer, Consumer Services

19 Victoria Gardens
New Mills
High Peak
SK12 4BC

28th December 2014

Your ref: 97259350

V Severs
Nestlé Consumer Service
P0 Box 203
York
YO1 1XY

Dear V Severs

Thank you for your letter.

Where on earth did you get the idea that I requested Quality Street advertising material from you? I wrote to you requesting the correct pronunciation of the name Nestlé, and enquired as to whether or not you manufactured Affreyeymin. Please deal with this request as soon as possible as I really am anxious to obtain a supply of the aforementioned confectionary.

Regarding what you say about the pronunciation of Nestlé; it seems to me that if you can imagine I sent you a letter requesting Quality Street advertising material you can just as easily make a mistake regarding the pronunciation of Nestlé. This being the case so I am seeking a second opinion from the Oxford University Press before I settle the bet.

Sincerely

T Ravenscroft (Mr)

**Nestlé Consumer Service**
P0 Box 203
York
YO1 1XY

3rd January 2015

Mr T Ravenscroft
19 Victoria Gardens
New Mills
High Peak
SK12 4BC

OUR REF 97260387

Dear Mr Ravenscroft

Thank you for your recent letter.

May we first apologise for our administration error and for the information that was accidently sent to you.

We can confirm that the correct pronunciation of our company is 'Ness-lay'.

Also the goods which you have enquired about, namely Affreymin, are not manufactured by our company.

We are sorry you were disappointed with our reply and you felt you had to contact us further. We hope you continue to enjoy our products, meanwhile thank you once again for taking the trouble to write to us.

Yours sincerely

V Severs (Miss)
Administration Officer, Consumer Services

19 Victoria Gardens
New Mills
High Peak
SK12 4BC

6th January 2015

Your ref 97260387

V Severs
Nestlé Consumer Service
P0 Box 203
York
YO1 1XY

Dear V Severs

Further to my request for a supplier of Affreyeymin.

On a recent visit to a local Chinese restaurant I asked the waiter if he'd ever heard of Affreyeymin. He smiled, and in much better English than the London waiter had spoken, told me that it was more than possible that his countryman had meant 'After Eight Mints', and that due to his imperfect diction it had come out sounding like 'Affreyeymin'. The local waiter also said that when one is in a fish and chipshop and the Chinese gentleman behind the counter apparently says 'sore finger', in reality he is asking if you would like salt and vinegar on your fish supper. I must say this all seems a bit fanciful to me, but do you think it possible he could be right?

I am still waiting to hear from the Oxford University Press regarding the pronunciation of

Nestlé, but I am sure they will come down on my side, so I'm hanging on to the £50 for the time being.

Sincerely

T Ravenscroft (Mr)

## NO REPLY!

****

19 Victoria Gardens
New Mills
High Peak
SK12 4BC

2nd January 2015

J Heinz
Hayes Park
Hayes
Middlesex
UB4 8AL

Dear H J Heinz

It might be argued with some justification that the following event took place due to an unfortunate coincidence, that had my youngest son Oscar's tortoise been where it should have been, i.e. in its box, and not on the kitchen floor, it would never have happened. Having said that, it in no way absolves H J Heinz from its part in the tragic affair.

The debacle happened on the night it was my wife's turn to compile the questions for her weekly W.I. quiz, and I was helping her, aided by my very good friend the internet. The Trivia Quiz on the H J Heinz website looked to be a promising source, and I picked out a couple of likely questions. "Try this for size," I said to my wife, and read out the first of them. "'What's the best way to get Heinz Tomato Ketchup to exit the iconic bottle?' To which the answer is: 'To release Heinz Tomato Ketchup from its glass bottle with extra speed, apply a firm tap to the spot marked '57' on the neck label."

My eldest son Marcus was seated at the kitchen

table at the time, a bottle of your tomato ketchup in hand prior to shaking it liberally on his haddock, as per usual. On hearing me he took the advice to heart and gave the bottle a hearty thump in the prescribed manner. The second of the trivia questions I had picked out was 'At what speed does Heinz Tomato Ketchup exit the iconic bottle', the answer being 'Ketchup exits the iconic glass bottle at 0.028 miles per hour'. I have no way of determining if this information is correct, but what I do know is that the bottle, having left Marcus's grasp when he thumped the bottom of it, travelled a great deal faster than 0.028 miles per hour - probably at about 100 miles per hour I would guess - narrowly missing the cat before smashing into the aforementioned tortoise, breaking its shell (and Oscar's heart.)

In view of this I would respectfully ask you to remove the question from your Trivia Quiz to prevent such an accident ever happening again. Whether or not you wish to compensate Oscar for his loss is a matter for your conscience. (The sauce bottle didn't seem to have done any further damage to the tortoise, apart from an initial wobble when it set off walking, and Oscar managed to repair its shell with tortoise-coloured masking tape. But it will never be the same of course.)

Sincerely

T Ravenscroft (Mr)

## NO REPLY!

****

19 Victoria Gardens
New Mills
High Peak
SK12 4BC

Little Dish
Astley House
33 Notting Hill Gate
London
W11 3JQ

Dear Little Dish

For some time I have included your excellent Little Dish Alphabet Spaghetti Bolognese in my four-year-old son Oscar's diet, along with his fish (although not of course at the same time). This provides him with a nourishing meal whilst at the same time allowing him the opportunity to improve his language skills whilst he is eating it. What could be better? Well for one thing it could be quite a lot better if your soup didn't have letter 'Ks' in it: because it wasn't long before - shown the way and egged on by his older brothers - that young Oscar tired of forming the words I'd taught him, such as 'cat' and 'dog', and started composing words such as 'cock', and 'knickers', along with words for masturbation and procreation containing the letter 'K'.

Thankfully Oscar's brothers have yet to learn the word 'dyke' or I might have an upset au pair on my hands, in addition to a wife who is threatening to ban your Alphabet Spaghetti Bolognese from the house if our son continues with his pornographic prose.

Short of standing by and allowing my wife to

carry out her threat I am struggling to come up with an answer to the problem. Maybe you at Little Dish can offer a suggestion? Short, that is, of going through the soup with a fine toothcomb and removing the Ks before it reaches the table, which I have already tried and found to be too messy, in addition to it by no means being 100% effective as you can't make out some of the letters while they're still covered in soup.

Sincerely

T Ravenscroft (Mr)

little dish
PROPER FOOD FOR KIDS

**Little Dish**
**33 Astley House**
**Notting Hill Gate**
**London**
**W11 3JQ**

29/01/15

Mr T Ravenscroft
19 Victoria Gardens
New Mills
High Peak
SK12 4BC

Dear Mr Ravenscroft

Thank you for your letter dated the 14th of January. It is great to hear that you find our Alphabet Pasta Bolognese to be nourishing as well as a great way for your son Oscar to improve his language skills. However, we are very sorry to hear that your son's discovery of the letter K in our Alphabet Pasta Bolognese has resulted in his using a plethora of less-favourable words.

After careful consideration from the Team and I, we feel that the 'K' should remain in the range not only for Oscar's own personal development but that removing the letter 'K' from our dish would mean that it really wouldn't be 'Alphabet Pasta' as it would only contain 25 letters. Furthermore, Oscar will need the letter 'K' to spell 'Kitkat' should he ever need to take a break.

We believe that for as long as little Oscar and his brothers join forces, there is absolutely no limit to their ability, and what they can create. We hope in time Oscar uses the pasta to create less crude words such as:

Khamsin – A dry hot local wind
Kavakava – A crop of the western pacific
Kumquats – A group of small fruit bearing trees

Thank you again for your letter and please accept our apologies for your experience and enjoy a free Little Dish meal on us with the voucher enclosed.

Yours Sincerely

Emma Brocksom
Customer Care - Little Dish

19 Victoria Gardens
New Mills
High Peak
SK12 4BC

4th February 2015

Emma Brocksom
Customer Care - Little Dish
Astley House
33 Notting Hill Gate
London
W11 3JQ

Dear Emma Brocksom

Thank you for the reply to my letter, which you seemed to treat with a little more levity than I would expect from a company with whom I am spending in excess of £200 a year. A little more concern for a worried parent would be appreciated.

Nor do my sons need any help in coming up with words containing the letter 'K', thank you very much; they already have more than enough flair for this, having proved the point since I last wrote to you by coming up with the phrase 'I'd like to fuck Kim Kardashian'. (This, incidentally, took two helpings of Alphabet Pasta Bolognese, as there were only three 'Ks' in the first one opened and they had to open another one, none of my sons possessing the wit to settle for 'I'd like to shag Kim Kardashian'.)

Might I suggest leaving the 'Ks' out of your product and calling it 'K-less Alphabet Pasta Bolognese', or even 'Alphabet Pasta Bolognese without Ks'? Anything to remove the risk of aiding and abetting the making up of filthy words by your customers' offspring.

Sincerely

T Ravenscroft (Mr)

****

19 Victoria Gardens
New Mills
High Peak
SK12 4BC

17th November 2014

Consumer Services
KitKat
Haxby Road
York
YO91 1XY.

Dear KitKat

Tesco's online shopping facility let me down the other day - not for the first time I might add - when quite inexplicably they included seven bars of KitKat in my weekly shop instead of the seven tins of KiteKat, which has been my regular order for the past three years. I got on to Tesco as soon as I made the discovery. They came up with the pathetic excuse that they are training new staff. I told them that if they were to perhaps pay their staff a little more than the minimum they can get away with then it would be more than possible that they wouldn't have to train new staff every five minutes, as the staff they already had might be inspired to stay with them a little longer. However I don't expect they will have taken too much notice of me, if past experience is anything to go by.

Anyway, there I was with a hungry cat and without the means to stem its hunger and no immediate way of stemming it, as I live miles from the shops. I was about to give Graham a treat and share a tin of Iceland's Fray Bentos Meatballs in Tomato Sauce with him when I remembered that the last time I did this - the week Tesco had delivered only six tins of Kitekat instead of the seven ordered - I had the devil's own job getting him back on the Kitekat again when the new supply arrived the following day.

At that point, perhaps because the word KitKat is only an 'e' short of the word KiteKat, I had the inspired idea of trying Graham with a KitKat, a bar of which I fortunately had to hand. I say 'inspired' because he wolfed down every last morsel! Then sat there licking his lips and paws the way cats do, and mewing for more.

Three days and three more KitKats on and I swear that Graham is moving a lot better - he is a very old cat and has arthritis - but it could be just my imagination.

Have you ever heard of cats who like KitKat before? Nobody who I have mentioned it to has.

Sincerely

T Ravenscroft (Mr)

PURINA
PetCareteam

**Purina PetCare Team**
**PO Box 478**
**Horley**
**RH6 6DE**

19 Victoria Gardens
New Mills
High Peak
SK12 4BC

Tuesday, 09 December 2014

Our Reference 02581149

Dear Mr. Ravenscroft

Thank you for your letter regarding your cat Graham.

We were very interested to hear about Grahams interest in the kit kat bars which you have fed to him. It is certainly very unusual for a cat to enjoy sweet foods and not something that we hear about very often.

We wouldn't recommend feeding chocolate products to Graham as chocolate can be toxic to cats. As a general rule of thumb the darker the chocolate the more dangerous it is. As kit kats are milk chocolate and are just a thin layer Graham will be ok on this occasion, but we would advise avoiding feeding any chocolate in the future.

We certainly haven't heard any reports of kit kats easing the symptom of arthritis before so we think that this may be a happy coincidence.

We have enclosed some Felix cat treats for Graham to try as these will be better for him than kit kats. We hope he enjoys them.

Yours sincerely

Kim Elcock RVN
Vet Nurse
Purina PetCare Team

19 Victoria Gardens
New Mills
High Peak
SK12 4BC

12th December 2014

Kim Elcock RVN
Purina PetCare Team
PO Box 478
Horley
RH6 6DE

Your Reference 02581149

Dear Kim Elcock

Thank you for your letter and the helpful advice. In fact I had already stopped feeding Graham KitKats, not because I feared I might poison him (which of course I wasn't aware of until you informed me) but because since I wrote to you he has disgraced himself on three occasions. This is very un-Graham like, I can assure you. An educated guess told me it might have been the KitKats that were to blame.

I tried Graham with the Felix Crispies you sent but I'm afraid he turned his nose up at them. (I think if I were a cat I would have done the same, after having got used to KitKats!) However it isn't all bad news. I have currently got my three sons on a fish diet, thanks to The Cornish Fisherman, in an effort to improve their brains. A side effect of this will be that it also improves their health. As a further boost to their well-being I am trying to wean them off potato crisps, which they all eat like they're going out of fashion. With this in mind I got them to try, as an alternative, the Felix

Crispies. Two of my sons quite enjoyed them and even Oscar, the pickiest of my boys, said they were 'all right, but a bit fishy, and I think I'm getting enough fish at the moment if I can be honest with you, Dad.'

Anyway I intend to substitute Felix Crispies for potato crisps, especially as they work out cheaper per gram. My sons eat rather a lot of crisps so will no doubt be eating a lot of Felix Crispies. Do you do a discount for quantity?

Sincerely

T Ravenscroft (Mr)

## NO REPLY!

****

19 Victoria Gardens
New Mills
High Peak
SK12 4BC

8th February 2015

Pot Noodle
Croespenmaen Industrial Estate
Kendon
Crumlin
Gwent
NP11 3AG

Dear Pot Noodle

I have long been a fan of your 'plastic pots of paradise' - your description of course, but one with which I absolutely concur - and can't imagine anything better to fill a gap, whether employed as a snack or a superior light lunch. You must feel justifiably proud to have come up with something so satisfyingly good at such an eminently affordable price. I've dined on all your pots over the years and Chicken and Mushroom is my unqualified favourite. But did you know that with a little tweaking to your recipe even your Chicken and Mushroom can be improved?

There may of course be other ways, but I have found that the biggest step up in quality is achieved by binning a quarter of the contents of the pot - a criminal waste, I know, but you have to make room for the additional ingredients - and replacing it with an ounce and a half of shredded free-range roast chicken, half a teaspoonful of truffle oil, half a teaspoonful of tomato puree, a chopped anchovy, half an ounce of Tesco Roasted Red Pepper Flakes, two chopped Kalamata Greek black olives, a pinch of saffron, and a pinch of salt. (I am aware that you have reduced the salt content of Pot Noodles to meet our Nanny State's healthy-eating guidelines, but I always put back in what you have left out anyway: if feeling a bit unhealthier to make your pot noodles taste better is the price one must pay, then so be it.)

Please feel at liberty to try my recipe for yourselves. By all means introduce it to your range if you find it agreeable, as I'm sure you will.

Sincerely

T Ravenscroft (Mr)

19 Victoria Gardens
New Mills
High Peak
SK12 4BC

9th February 2015

Pot Noodle
Croespenmaen Industrial Estate
Kendon
Crumlin
Gwent
NP11 3AG

Dear Pot Noodle

Reference my letter of yesterday. Hold everything. I've tried the ounce and a half of shredded free-range roast chicken, half a teaspoonful of truffle oil, half a teaspoonful of tomato puree, a chopped anchovy, half an ounce of Tesco Roasted Red Pepper Flakes, two chopped Kalamata Greek black olives, a pinch of saffron, and a pinch of salt *without* the Pot Noodle and it's even better than it is with it. Sorry about that.

****

19 Victoria Gardens
New Mills
High Peak
SK12 4BC

24th November 2014

Mr Kipling Cakes
Kingfisher Business Park
London Road
Stroud
GL5 2BY

Dear Mr Kipling

I recently bought a packet of your Mr Kipling Exceedingly Good 6 Bakewell Slices. They were Exceedingly Bad. No, that's unfair, but they were certainly a little disappointing.

I have the advantage of being a Derbyshire man, born not too far from Bakewell, home of the famous Bakewell Pudding (the forerunner of the Bakewell Tart), and as such know what a Bakewell Tart should taste like. I'm afraid yours doesn't taste anything like it.

Of course the tarts I was brought up on, baked on the premises of local shops, were more or less home made, and whilst I realise that you are making your tarts by the million, and that a reduction in standards is the bedfellow of mass production, I would suggest that to call your tarts Exceedingly Good is overstating their excellence somewhat. Maybe you could consider calling them something more modest, something achievable? 'Mr Kipling's Quite Decent Bakewell Slices' for example. Although even that description is pushing it a bit. Perhaps 'Mr

Kipling's Not Bad Bakewell Slices'? That would seem about right - not only is it a bit self effacing, which is never a bad thing in my view, but it would also stop potential customers from building their hopes up too much, with the consequent risk of disappointing them.

Sincerely

T Ravenscroft (Mr)

PREMIER FOODS

Mr T Ravenscroft
19 Victoria Gardens
New Mills
High Peak
SK12 4BC

04/12/2014

Reference No: 283806

Dear Mr Ravenscroft

Please accept our apologies for the problem you have had with Mr Kipling Bakewell Tart. Thank you for bringing the matter to our attention.

If you could kindly supply us with the codes from the packaging we will write and reimburse you.

The codes we would like are the bar code, the best before dates and the codes printed after the best before date, which can be found on either side of the packaging.

Please be assured that all the details of your complaint have been passed onto our Quality Assurance Department for their attention.

Thank you once again for taking the time to contact us.

Yours sincerely,

Rupinder Singh
Consumer Relations Advisor
Enclosed PPPS

**Careline Services, Premier Foods 250 Gunnersbury Avenue London W4 5QB**

19 Victoria Gardens
New Mills
High Peak
SK12 4BC

18th December 2014

Rupinder Singh
Premier Foods
250 Gunnersbury Avenue
London
W4 5QB

Your Reference No: 283806

Dear Rupinder Singh

Thank you for your letter, although in truth it seems to be nothing more than a standard reply, which, true to its function, makes no attempt to address the points raised.

In fact you seem to have got the wrong end of the stick entirely. I was not complaining about the quality or otherwise of your Mr Kipling Exceedingly Good Bakewell Slices; I was merely pointing out that it is a bit presumptuous to say that they are 'exceedingly good', when clearly they are not - or at least not when compared to the Bakewell Tarts and Puddings to be had from the shop in Bakewell that originated them.

Perhaps it is because, as someone from the subcontinent, you are not familiar with the history of the iconic Bakewell Tart? In which case an analogy, paying homage to your ethnicity, might be appropriate. Allow me to offer 'To call a Mr Kipling Bakewell Slice 'exceedingly good', when comparing it to an original Bakewell Tart, is a bit like comparing curried cat food to the finest Kashmiri Lamb Rogan Josh'.

There, I hope I've cleared that up satisfactorily.

Finally I would urge you to give serious thought to adopting my suggestion of calling your product 'Mr Kipling's Not Bad Bakewell Slices'. I am sure you wouldn't lose any sales by doing this, and would probably gain some; many people in the UK preferring honesty to hype.

Sincerely

T Ravenscroft (Mr)

PREMIER FOODS

Mr T Ravenscroft
19 Victoria Gardens
New Mills
High Peak
SK12 4BC

09/01/2015

Reference No: 283806

Dear Mr Ravenscroft

Thank you for your comments regarding our Mr Kipling Exceedingly Good Bakewell Slices.

It is always good to receive feedback from our customers and we appreciate the time taken to contact us.

We can confirm that your comments have now been forwarded on to our marketing department for their information.

Yours sincerely,

Rupinder Singh
Consumer Relations Advisor

**Careline Services, Premier Foods 250 Gunnersbury Avenue London W4 5QB**

****

19 Victoria Gardens
New Mills
High Peak
SK12 4BC

2nd December 2014

Go Vietnam!
Arrow Business Park
England House
Brighton
BN7 4GH

Dear Go Vietnam!

I plan to holiday in Vietnam this year with my wife and our two dogs Castor and Pollux. (The dogs have been vaccinated and a Vietnam International Health Certificate and a Rabies Certificate obtained).

However, since conceiving the idea I have learned that the Vietnamese eat dogs as part of their menu; and whilst I have no objection to people eating dogs I don't want them eating my dogs. (It also, incidentally, explained to me why fans of my football team, referring to our Vietnamese winger, shout 'He'll shoot, He'll score, He'll eat your Labrador', which had always puzzled me.)

From the same source I also learned that in Vietnam dog meat is believed to bring good luck. All I can say to that is that it doesn't bring the dogs much in the way of good luck!

Further investigations led me to discover that not only is the eating of dog meat prevalent in Vietnam but that the demand for dog meat for the local restaurant trade is such that dogs are often snatched off the street. Naturally this causes me great concern. It also occurs to me that as my two St Bernard's represent a 'meatier' example of dog than is perhaps normally to be found on the streets of Vietnam, that they would be a particularly attractive target for any would be dog-snatcher.

Accepting of course that you can't give any guarantees, I was wondering if you could help me; first by reassuring me that dog snatching isn't as rampant as I have been led to believe, and secondly by perhaps suggesting areas of Vietnam where the snatching of dogs off the street is not a problem?

I thank you in expectation of your reply.

Sincerely

T Ravenscroft (Mr)

# Go Vietnam!

T Ravenscroft
19 Victoria Gardens
New Mills
High Peak
SK12 4BC

12th December 2014

OUR REF: 1884/CF

Dear Mr Ravenscroft

You are correct in your assumption that in Vietnam the locals eat dog, both in normal restaurants and in speciality dog food restaurants. There are however many hundreds of restaurants that don't serve dog and you will have no trouble finding these.

Reference dog-snatching, I have to admit that it does happen. The best advice I can offer is to keep your dogs on a short leash and don't walk them in the hours of darkness.

Both our Saigon & Beach and our Northern Highlights holidays would ensure that you never need go anywhere near a restaurant that serves dog.

If there is anything else I can do for you, please ask.

Yours sincerely

Clark Fleetwood
Go Vietnam!

**Go Vietnam! Arrow Business Park England House Brighton BN7 4GH**

19 Victoria Gardens
New Mills
High Peak
SK12 4BC

12 April 2015

Clark Fleetwood
Go Vietnam!
Arrow Business Park
England House
Brighton
BN7 4GH

Dear Clark

Just a line or two to thank you for a lovely holiday in Vietnam. Thanks to your guidance we managed to steer well clear of any restaurants that had dog on the menu (although we did go in one that had cat on the menu, which I certainly wasn't expecting, but apparently cats are eaten over there too. We stuck with the chicken.)

However I did eat dog. In the form of a dog kebab. The street vendor told me it was pork, but I was informed by a fellow guest at the hotel that street vendors always say this because if they told you it was dog you wouldn't buy it. The following day I challenged the street vendor about this and he owned up. I must admit that I had found the dog kebab to be quite tasty, more like wild boar than your standard pork, so I ordered another. It was just as good. Castor and Pollux looked on with eyes filled with longing whilst I ate it, whilst the street vendor looked with eyes full of longing at Castor and Pollux, all three of them hungrily smacking their lips, the dogs quite oblivious to the fact that I was eating one of their oriental cousins. When they die, I may eat them.

Anyway, thanks again for contributing to a lovely holiday.

Sincerely

T Ravenscroft (Mr)

****

19 Victoria Gardens
New Mills
High Peak
SK12 4BC

5th January 2015

Asda
Great Wilson Street
Leeds
LS11 5AD

Dear Asda

I have long been a fan of your Smartprice Tomato Soup and must by now have consumed hundreds of gallons of it. I prefer your version of tomato soup to the tomato soup of other manufacturers, probably because I am a man who likes his tomato soup to be as tomatoey as possible, and tomato soups don't come any more tomatoey than Asda's, and I've tried them all.

I was therefore surprised on finding that the soup I had for lunch yesterday was distinctly less tomatoey than I have come to expect. Why is this? Could it be that you've changed your tomato supplier, with a consequential lowering in quality? Perhaps you have switched from succulent Spanish tomatoes to more astringent English ones, with the same outcome? Or maybe it's because your man whose job it is to feed in the tomatoes is falling down on the job? Whatever it is, it has made your tomato soup less tomatoey.

Sincerely

T Ravenscroft (Mr)

ASDA
SAVING
YOU MONEY EVERY DAY

Our Ref: 150108-000577

Mr T Ravenscroft
19 Victoria Gardens
New Mills
High Peak
SK12 4BC

09 January 2015

Dear Mr Ravenscroft

Thanks for taking the time to get in contact with me about the Asda smartprice tomato soup you have purchased from one of our Asda stores.

I am sorry that when you had the soup for your lunch it tasted less tomatoey than before. I can appreciate why you are disappointed by this, especially as you've been a fan of this for sometime.

We expect all the products we sell to be of real quality. I'm pleased you've taken the time to bring this to my attention as your feedback is vital for us to continue to improve our product quality.

I have passed your feedback onto our buying team and asked for this to be raised with the supplier, this will be closely monitored with changes made where needed to improve.

Yours sincerely

Sophie Workman
Asda Service Team

**Customer Services ASDA Stores Ltd Great Wilson Street Leeds LS11 5AD**

19 Victoria Gardens
New Mills
High Peak
SK12 4BC

13th January 2015

Your Ref: 150108-000577
Sophie Workman
Asda Service Team
Asda
Great Wilson Street
Leeds
LS11 5AD

Dear Sophie Workman

Sorry, I made a mistake; it was a tin of your Smartprice Oxtail Soup that I had - I opened it in error under the impression it was Tomato. It *was* quite tomatoey though.

To make up for my wasting your valuable time might I be presumptuous enough to offer you a little help with your grammar? The words 'Asda smartprice tomato soup' should *all* be capitalised. It should be 'some time', not 'sometime' and 'on to' not 'onto'. And your final sentence would be much clearer if it read: 'I have passed your feedback onto our buying team and asked for this to be raised with the supplier; this will be closely monitored, with changes made where a need to improve is indicated.'

No need to write to thank me.

Sincerely

T Ravenscroft (Mr)

****

19 Victoria Gardens
New Mills
High Peak
SK12 4BC

20th November 2014

Ye Olde Oak Foods Ltd
PO Box 801
Halifax
HX1 9PS

Dear Ye Olde Oak Foods

My family have been enjoying your tins of 8 Ye Olde Oak Foods Hot Dogs for quite a few years and I have nothing but praise for them. However I must complain about the last can we opened as inside were not 8 Ye Olde Oak Foods Hot Dogs, as one would expect, but 9. You might say that this should not be a cause for complaint, particularly as I have already said that we have been enjoying them for years. However, as you are no doubt well aware, if there are 8 hot dogs in your can there isn't room for a ninth hot dog. This being the case, the extra one had been crammed in, causing it to partially disintegrate, along with the four other hot dogs it had come into contact with.

Whilst not being ungrateful for the extra hot dog I would much rather have done without it; principally because, due to the collateral damage, the hot dogs didn't look as attractive on the plate as they usually do, but also because it set two of my sons, Marcus and Henry, squabbling over which of them got the extra one (I'd given them a day off from fish and they seemed determined to make the most of it). The argument turned into a fight, during which Marcus inflicted a black eye on his smaller brother.

With this in mind I very much hope that in future you will be a bit more careful about how many hot dogs you put in your cans, desirable though they are.

Sincerely

T Ravenscroft (Mr)

**Ye Olde Oak Foods Ltd**
**No 2 Warehouse**
**The Wharf**
**Sowerby Bridge**
**HX6 2AG**

Our ref: 43526
26th November 2014

Mr Ravenscroft
19 Victoria Gardens
New Mills
High Peak
SK12 4BC

Dear Mr Ravenscroft

We were extremely sorry to hear that you have experienced a problem with one of our products.

We pride ourselves on our high standards and we will look into this matter.

Please accept the enclosed voucher's and we hope you will still continue to purchase the Ye Olde Oak brand.

Many thanks

Vickie Wadsworth
UK Sales Office Manager

19 Victoria Gardens
New Mills
High Peak
SK12 4BC

4th December 2014

Vickie Wadsworth
Ye Olde Oak Foods Ltd
No 2 Warehouse
The Wharf
Sowerby Bridge
HX6 2AG

Your ref: 43526

Dear Vickie

Thank you for the 3 x 1 Asda vouchers. Unfortunately I won't be able to use them as I am banned from Asda following a fracas with one of their checkout girls who tried to cheat me. Could you please replace them with vouchers that I can use at Tesco or Iceland? Where I am still welcome.

When you have looked into the matter I would be interested to learn the findings of your investigations as obviously I am keen not to get another 9 sausage can after what happened the last time.

Sincerely

T Ravenscroft (Mr)

PS. In the meantime we have opened another can of 8 Ye Olde Oak Foods Hot Dogs and it was perfect in both quality and complement of sausages.

**Ye Olde Oak Foods Ltd**
**No 2 Warehouse**
**The Wharf**
**Sowerby Bridge**
**HX6 2AG**

Our ref: 43526
21st December 2014

Mr Ravenscroft
19 Victoria Gardens
New Mills

Dear Mr Ravenscroft

Please accept the enclosed Tesco Gift Card to the value of £3. Many thanks.

Vickie Wadsworth
UK Sales Office Manager

****

19 Victoria Gardens
New Mills
High Peak
SK12 4BC

26th November 2014

Subway
Mill Court
Great Shelford
Cambridge
CB22 5LD

Dear Subway

Every time my wife and I visit a Subway we each have a 9-Grain Honey Oat Six Inch Sub. Or we would each have a 9-Grain Honey Oat Six Inch Sub if your counter assistant was a bit less cavalier with the use of the bread knife. As things stand it is far from uncommon, on cutting the 12 inch long bread into two halves, for him to end up with one half longer than the other. Often he is in error by as much as half an inch, which results in him ending up not with two six inch subs but one five and a half inch sub and one six and a half inch sub. *And it is always me who ends up with the five and a half inch one.*

If we both had the same sub it would not be a problem; I could simply take the larger one, or at least take turns at having the larger one. Alternatively we could buy a 12 inch sub and have the counter assistant cut it in half, in which case I could still take the larger half in my turn. However I always have a Turkey & Ham Sub whilst my wife, employing the woman's prerogative of not being able to make up her mind when faced with a choice, eventually has something else, often an Italian BMT Sub or a Chicken & Chorizo Sub, but whatever it is it isn't a Turkey & Ham Sub, which is the only one I like.

I have tried altering my position in the queue relative to my wife. But whichever position I choose, to the right of her (in front of her in the queue) or to the left of her, (behind her in the queue) Sod's Law always kicks in and she gets the longer sub. It is most annoying, as you can well imagine. You might think that perhaps I need only draw the attention of the counter assistant as to the disparity between the two halves of bread before he puts the filling on, and request that he puts ham and turkey on the larger half and chicken and Chorizo on the smaller, but that is not the way of a gentleman.

Have you any suggestions? Other than kick Subway into touch and go to a McDonalds, an establishment - although not to be recommended to all but the desperate - where the size of your lunch doesn't depend upon the assistant's dexterity with the bread knife?

Sincerely

T Ravenscroft (Mr)

**SUBWAY REALTY LIMITED**

19 Victoria Gardens
New Mills
High Peak
SK12 4BC

1st December 2014

Dear Mr Ravenscroft

**RE:** Customer letter reference: 3460579

Thank you for taking the time to contact the SUBWAY© brand.

I am sorry to learn that your visit was not what you expected it to be.

Our customers provide us with valuable input, which we use to improve our operations. As part of our commitment to our customers, I would like to share your comments with the owner of the SUBWAY© store that you visited. As every SUBWAY© store is owned and operated independently, he or she will then be able to address directly your concerns.

Could you please specify the exact address of the store you visited, using the store locator on our website www.subway.co.uk?

Thank you in advance and kind regards,

Customer Care
SUBWAY© UK & Ireland

**Chaston House, Mill Court, Hinton Way, Great Shelford, Cambridge, CB22 5LD**

19 Victoria Gardens
New Mills
High Peak
SK12 4BC

4th December 2014

Subway
Mill Court
Great Shelford
Cambridge
CB22 5LD

Your Customer letter reference: 3460579

Dear Customer Care, Subway

Reference your letter of the 1st December. My wife and I visit a least half a dozen Subways in the vicinity. The problem that I outlined is endemic in all of them and not, as you would seem to think, in just the one.

I have no wish to be unpleasant about this in order to get satisfaction - it is not my way - but I really do think you would be well advised to take the matter a bit more seriously than you have taken it thus far. When all is said and done, by serving up to your customers a sub of anything less than six inches in length you are in effect cheating them, not to mention breaching the Trades Description Act.

Fortunately there is an easy way out for you. My friend Mr Atkins, a keen amateur inventor of some note - he is the inventor of the silent bagpipes - has come up with an item of apparatus that will solve the problem once and for all. I have called it the SUBCUTTER© and enclose a drawing of same, which is self explanatory. Using this ingenious device it would be impossible for your counter assistants to serve up anything other than a six inch sub.

Mr Atkins says that the cost of the SUBCUTTER©, in aluminium with a mild steel guillotine, guaranteed for twelve months, would be in the region of £10 each, delivered. A small price to pay for complete customer satisfaction I would say.

Sincerely

T Ravenscroft (Mr)

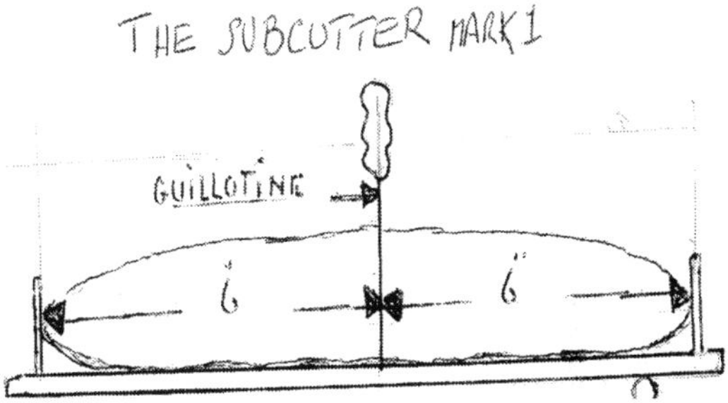

**SUBWAY REALTY LIMITED**

Mr T Ravenscroft
19 Victoria Gardens
New Mills
SK12 4BC

8th December 2014

Dear Mr Ravenscroft

**RE:** Comment ID 3460579

Thank you for taking the time to contact the SUBWAY© brand.

As every SUBWAY© is owned and operated independently, I would need to know which stores you have experienced this issue in so that I am able to pass the feedback to the owners of those stores.

There is equipment in place for the staff to use already and this is why we would need to know the list of stores you have been to, so that the franchisees are able to take this up with their staff.

For Mr Atkins Subcutter device you will need to contact our purchasing team, please visit their website at www.eipc.eu to find out more.

Kindest regards,

Customer Care
SUBWAY© UK & Ireland

**Chaston House, Mill Court, Hinton Way, Great Shelford, Cambridge, CB22 5LD**

19 Victoria Gardens
New Mills
High Peak
SK12 4BC

11th December 2014

Subway
Mill Court
Great Shelford
Cambridge
CB22 5LD

Re: Comment ID3460579

Dear Customer Care, Subway

Reference the statement in your letter of 8th December that 'there is equipment in place for the staff to use already'.

During the years I have been dining at SUBWAY© I must have visited at least twenty branches at one time or another. I have never once seen any of your counter staff using a chainsaw to cut your bread rolls. Nor have I seen them using a machete. Nor a cutlass, nor a pair of scissors, nor a laser beam. Nor, for that matter, have I seen them using any equipment similar to my friend Mr Atkins's SUBCUTTER© (pat pending) which would do the job to perfection.

No, the fact is that the only equipment I have ever seen your counter assistants using is a bread knife. With it they first slice the roll in half widthwise. Then they sometimes slice it in half lengthwise, but more often than not slice it lengthwise into two parts, neither of which is a half. Which is what I complained to you about in the first place.

So what is this 'equipment' you refer too, which I seem to have missed? And why aren't the counter staff using it? And don't ask me for a list of the SUBWAY© outlets I have visited where they aren't using it; they aren't using it anywhere.

The aforementioned Mr Atkins is most disappointed about your lack of interest in his SUBCUTTER© (pat pending). He says he thinks he will be able to do it for £9, if that is any help to you.

Sincerely

T Ravenscroft (Mr)

NO REPLY!

****

19 Victoria Gardens
New Mills
High Peak
SK12 4BC

8th January 2015

Customer Service Department
Wm Morrison Supermarkets PLC
Hilmore House
Gain Lane
Bradford
BD3 7DL

Dear Morrisons

I am a big fan of Subway, but having fallen out with them on a point of principle I am no longer able to enjoy my weekly six inch sub at one of their outlets. This being the case I thought I would have a go at making one myself. I plumped for my usual choice, a turkey & ham (proper turkey and ham, not Bernard Matthews Turkey Ham) with cheese and honey mustard sauce. All was going well until I opened the packet of Morrisons Cheese Slices I purchased for the cheese element of my sub, when to my amazement, not to mention disappointment, I found them to be full of holes!

I have no idea why should this be. Whenever I have had your cheese slices in the past they have always passed muster (I'm sure I would have noticed if they'd had holes in them), but holes in them, some of them quite large holes, there were. Maybe you have mice?

Fortunately it didn't affect the taste of my home-made sub - although the holes made it that bit less cheesy I suppose - but I thought I had better point it out to you in the hope that you should think it prudent to have a word with your quality control people so they can take steps to prevent your selling any more cheese slices with holes in them.

Sincerely

T Ravenscroft (Mr)

MORRISONS

26 January 2015

Our Ref: 02234380/AB

Mr T Ravenscroft
19 Victoria Gardens
New Mills
High Peak
SK12 4BC

Dear Mr Ravenscroft

Thank you for contacting us.

I was most concerned to learn of your disappointment with a recent purchase of some Morrisons Cheese Slices. Please accept my most sincere apologies for this.

At Morrisons our aim is only to offer good quality value for money products and our dedicated Buyers work closely with our suppliers to ensure that this aim is met. Therefore it is most regrettable that on this occasion your purchase gave cause for dissatisfaction.

As we would never want our customers to be dissatisfied with any purchase made from us, please accept the enclosed shopping voucher to reimburse you for your purchase and as a gesture of goodwill with our compliments.

Yours sincerely

Daniel Wilkinson
Customer Services Advisor.

**Wm Morrison Supermarkets PLC, Hilmore House, Gain Lane, Bradford, BD3 7DL**

19 Victoria Gardens
New Mills
High Peak
SK12 4BC

16th February 2015

Daniel Wilkinson
Customer Service Advisor
Wm Morrison Supermarkets PLC
Gain Lane
Bradford
BD3 7DL

Dear Morrisons

Thank you for the £5 voucher. I was going to return it, as since corresponding with you I have discovered that the cheese slices I purchased from you were Gruyere cheese, a cheese that apparently is supposed to have holes in it! (Although why people should want cheese with holes in it remains a mystery to me. Maybe you could enlighten me?)

However, I had second thoughts, as in the meantime I had tried some of your Decadent Belgian Double Chocolate Fudge Cake, which turned out to be far too rich for my taste - possibly the Decadent Belgian who made it was a bit *too* decadent - and gave me constipation. So I spent the voucher on some of your Dulcoease Stool Softener Capsules. (Which worked admirably, I am happy to report. Maybe you could do them in a dual pack, with your Decadent Belgian Double Chocolate Fudge Cake?)

Sincerely
T Ravenscroft (Mr)

****

19 Victoria Gardens
New Mills
High Peak
SK12 4BC

17th December 2014

The Editor
Your Derbyshire
Derbyshire County Council
County Hall
Matlock
DE4 3AG

Dear Editor

Reference the December issue of *Your Derbyshire* magazine, which somewhat belatedly dropped through my letter box yesterday. One must hope that the householders of Derbyshire pay their Council Tax with greater attention given to the date it is due.

Ever mindful of the austerity measures that have dictated the current economic climate I was drawn to the article 'Five tips to SAVE £s on festive food' on page 11. Tips 1 to 4 seem to make good sense and I intend to carry them out as best I can. However I couldn't make head or tail of the advice contained in Tip 5, Love Your Leftovers, which includes the sentence 'Panettone makes a lovely bread and butter pudding - why not serve it up with luxurious ice cream made from leftover Christmas pud?'

How on earth does one make ice cream from a Christmas pud? If there is a way it is beyond my wit to fathom out what it is, and I would be grateful if you could enlighten me as to what it is.

And perhaps you can include it in the next issue of your magazine, as I am quite sure there are many other people who will be similarly mystified.

Sincerely

T Ravenscroft (Mr)

DERBYSHIRE
County Council
Improving life for local people

Mr T Ravenscroft
19 Victoria Gardens
New Mills
High Peak
SK12 4BC

22 December 2014

Dear Mr Ravenscroft

Thank you for your letter dated 17 December about the December issue of *Your Derbyshire* which was scheduled to be delivered to all Derbyshire households from 8 December.

We're pleased to hear that you're interested in the article 'Five tips to save £s on festive food'. Sorry that the reference to the ice cream recipe was not as clear as it could have been.

The ice cream can simply be made by crumbling leftover Christmas pudding into Vanilla ice cream. There are many more money-saving food ideas so we hope you enjoy trying some of these for yourself. Some of these are enclosed with this letter.

Thank you for taking the time to write to us sharing your thoughts.

Yours faithfully

Joanne Beck
Communcations team.
Enc

**Derbyshire County Council, County Hall, Matlock, DE4 3AG**

19 Victoria Gardens
New Mills
High Peak
SK12 4BC

29th December 2014

Joanne Beck
Your Derbyshire
Derbyshire County Council
County Hall
Matlock
DE4 3AG

Dear Joanne Beck

Thank you for your reply.

If the money-saving food ideas you enclosed contain the same sort of thinking that informed your 'luxurious ice cream made from leftover Christmas pud' idea I don't think I'll be bothering, if it's all the same to you: adding Christmas pudding to vanilla ice cream doesn't make it Christmas Pudding Ice Cream no more than adding testicles to your auntie makes her your uncle, and I can't for the life of me understand why anyone would think it would.

As the December issue of *Your Derbyshire* was scheduled to be delivered to all Derbyshire households from 8 December I will in future be taking a leaf out of your scheduling book and sending you my Council Tax on the 8th of the month instead of the 1st, as demanded on your bill.

Merry Christmas and a Happy New Year.

Sincerely

T Ravenscroft (Mr)

****

19 Victoria Gardens
New Mills
High Peak
SK12 4BC

25th November 2014

Walkers Crisps
11 Burson Road
Beaumont Leys
Leicester
LE4 1BS

Dear Walkers Crisps

I wonder what you at Walkers think about the rubbish forever being bandied about in the newspapers and on TV a propos potato crisps being bad for you? My opinion, for what it is worth, is that they don't do you anything but good. (Incidentally, love your Pulled Pork in Sticky Barbecue Sauce crisps that won your recent 'Name a Flavour' competition: although, on reflection, perhaps a better expression than 'pulled pork' might have been used - in this part of the country the words 'pulled' and 'pork' in close proximity to each other has sexual connotations. Just thought I'd mention that; don't want to put the wrong idea into the minds of our growing youngsters, do we, they have quite enough wrong ideas as it is.)

But to get back to my contention that potato crisps are good for you. If testament to this were needed my three sons are living proof. All three of them have four bags a day that I am aware of, and quite possibly some bags that I'm not, and they don't seem to have come to any harm. If you wanted to nitpick I suppose that two of them,

Marcus and Henry, are what some people might call a bit overweight, and Oscar is what they might call a lot overweight, but these are growing lads we're talking about here, and if they happen to be growing out at a faster rate than they are growing up I'm sure it will all work out in the end. (As a point of interest, and an added bonus, eating plenty of potato crisps has resulted in Marcus finding his best position on the football field - he had visions of being a striker before his friends insisted in always picking him as the goalkeeper.)

I am aware that your man Gary Lineker has been quoted as saying - when asked to reconcile his fat cheques with the junk food-inspired fatness of the nation's youth - that one bag of crisps a day won't do you any harm. I am quite sure Gary is right (even if he would say that anyway). However, it has caused me to wonder just what *is* the best quantity of potato crisps per day to allow your children?

Sincerely

T Ravenscroft (Mr)

WALKERS

000794209

10 December 2014

Mr T Ravenscroft
19 Victoria Gardens
New Mills
High Peak
SK12 4BC

Dear Mr Ravenscroft

Thank you for writing to us.

We are so pleased you have taken the time out to tell us know how much you and your three sons like and enjoy our Walkers Crisps.

Your comments are really very special to us because it's your opinion that counts and is the reason for everything we do. I will be sharing your valued comments with our Marketing Team as I know they are always eager to learn what people think of our products.

With regards to the amount of packets your sons eat, I'm afraid we cannot advise you, perhaps speak to you local G P or a nutritionist.

Thanks again for writing and I hope you will all continue to enjoy our products for many years to come.

Yours sincerely

Elizabeth Harrison
Customer Services

**Walkers Snack Foods Ltd, PO Box 23, Leicester, LE4 1BS**

19 Victoria Gardens
New Mills
High Peak
SK12 4BC

11th December 2014

Elizabeth Harrison
Walkers Crisps
11 Burson Road
Beaumont Leys
Leicester
LE4 1BS

Your ref: 000794209A

Dear Elizabeth Harrison

Thank you for your reply. Excellent grammar, apart from one glaring mistake.

I was sorry to hear that you couldn't advise me on the amount of packets of crisps per day my sons might safely eat. However I did as you suggested and asked my GP. I can't remember his exact reply - and I've cut out all but two of the swear words - but it was something like 'None at all from what I saw of the size of the buggers when you got me out to the one you suspected of having acute appendicitis but it turned out to be chronic constipation brought on very probably by stuffing himself with too many packets of potato bloody crisps!' I pointed out to him that Oscar hadn't eaten any more crisps than his brothers, and that *they* hadn't got constipation, but my wife then informed me that Marcus did in fact have constipation, but not as bad as Oscar. (My other son Henry was functioning perfectly however, so far as I know, but I can't be 100% sure as at the time he was in hospital again.)

In view of the doctor's words I would be very interested in what you have to say about this; in particular anything about too many packets of crisps causing constipation.

Sincerely

T Ravenscroft (Mr)

000794209B

10 February 2015

Mr T Ravenscroft
19 Victoria Gardens
New Mills
High Peak
SK12 4BC

Dear Mr Ravenscroft

Thank you very much for your further letter.

I'm really very sorry but I'm afraid my response would be the same as before. I cannot advise you on any medical or nutritional queries you may have.

As I mentioned before, you could perhaps ask to speak to a nutritionist if you have concerns about your children's health or diet or would want more information about what foods to eat and how much.

Kind regards

Elizabeth Harrison
Customer Services

**Walkers Snack Foods Ltd, PO Box 23, Leicester, LE4 1BS**

19 Victoria Gardens
New Mills
High Peak
SK12 4BC

12th February 2014

Dear Elizabeth Harrison

Why am I not surprised by your answer? Especially as it has taken you five weeks to come up with it.

****

19 Victoria Gardens
New Mills
High Peak
SK12 4BC

21st November 2014

Green Giant
General Mills UK Ltd
PO Box 363
Uxbridge
UB8 1YT

Dear Green Giant

Here's a bit of good news that should make your jolly green giant even jollier!

I am a pigeon fancier of 20 years standing - quite a bit of it standing about waiting for my pigeons to return to the coop, actually. For all that time, and anxious to give my birds the best possible chance of victory in their races, I have fed them the best corn possible. Or so I thought. However a couple of weeks ago, due to circumstances beyond my control, I ran out of corn. It was too late to do anything about it, but fortunately my wife had a couple of cans of Green Giant Original Sweet Corn in the larder. I was a bit dubious about feeding it to my pigeons, as they mean the world to me, but needs must, as they say.

My pigeons ate it in their usual greedy manner, as pigeons are wont to do, and I thought no more about it. The following day I sent two of them over to Calais, France, to take part in a race. Not only did they come first and fourth in the race, but the pigeon that won - its first victory, by the way - broke the record for the trip. Naturally I wondered if it had anything to do with the Green Giant corn I fed them - men who race pigeons are always looking for an edge - but I doubted it and put it down to coincidence, especially as they'd only been fed with it the once. However, as an experiment, I thought I would feed some more of it to the pigeon I had selected for the next race on the pigeon racing calendar. As a control this pigeon was accompanied by a pigeon of equal merit that had been fed its usual corn. You can guess what happened. The Green Giant fed pigeon, which came in third overall (out of 346), beat the normally fed pigeon by almost five minutes, a huge margin in racing pigeon terms.

I now intend to feed all my pigeons with Green Giant Original Sweet Corn. As it is considerably more expensive than the corn I have used in the past, and as I have twenty-three pigeons, I am wondering if you could offer me a discount for quantity?

Sincerely

T Ravenscroft (Mr)

Mr T Ravenscroft
19 Victoria Gardens
New Mills
High Peak
SK12 4BC

3rd December 2014

Dear Mr Ravenscroft

Thank you for taking the time to contact our company.

We welcome your comments and are pleased that you are interested in our products. Please find a voucher as a goodwill gesture.

We appreciate your enthusiastic endorsement and hope you will continue to use and enjoy our products.

Yours sincerely,

A Bristow
**Consumer Relations**

Ref: 2014/12/01-0846GB
£5V

**Green Giant, PO Box 663, UB8 1YT, Uxbridge**

19 Victoria Gardens
New Mills
High Peak
SK12 4BC

12th December 2014

A Bristow
Customer Relations, Green Giant
General Mills UK Ltd
PO Box 363
Uxbridge
UB8 1YT

Dear A Bristow

Thank you for the £5 voucher.

Unfortunately there has been a tragedy since I last wrote to you. The original pigeon I fed with your Green Giant Original Sweet Corn has since died. The second pigeon I fed it to is thankfully still alive, but still very poorly; the vet gives it only a fifty-fifty chance.

The vet also said that Green Giant Original Sweet Corn was entirely the wrong sort of corn to feed to a pigeon, it being far too refined for the gullet of a bird, and was more than likely the reason for its demise, as in all probability it had waterlogged the bird's lungs.

Perhaps you should include this on your labelling, so that other pigeon fanciers don't make the same tragic mistake? Something like WARNING! DANGEROUS TO PIGEONS!! Perhaps with a little drawing of a pigeon with a red cross crossing it out (like you get on poison labels), as some people, pigeon fanciers amongst them, can't read. Or is that too stark a message? If you think it is I will try to think of something less blunt but will still get the message across - I am not a man who is short of ideas (although I am now a man who is short of a couple of pigeons!) Let me know.

I shall be buying a few cans of Green Giant Original Sweet Corn with the £5, but keeping it well clear of my pigeons.

Sincerely

T Ravenscroft (Mr)

## NO REPLY!

****

19 Victoria Gardens
New Mills
High Peak
SK12 4BC

18th December 2014

Boots Customer Care
PO Box 5300
Nottingham
NG90 1AA

Dear Boots

A short while ago I returned from a camping holiday in France. One day whilst there I did a bit of foraging in the woods for mushrooms and returned with a basket brim full of fungal bounty. Unfortunately I had no way of telling if the four types of mushroom I had collected were edible or otherwise. When I bemoaned this to a fellow (French) camper he informed me that I need only take the mushrooms along to the nearest chemist's shop, where they would not only identify them for me and tell me which were safe to eat, but would provide this service entirely free. I did, and it was.

On returning to England I got to wondering if British chemists provided the same service, and called in at my local Boots to enquire if this was the case. Your assistant told me that you didn't. This left me somewhat disappointed, as having had great success at foraging for mushrooms in France I had ambitions to do the same on home soil. However I was even more disappointed when your assistant, who had already treated my enquiry with scant interest, then proceeded to try to sell me a bottle of Mega-Mushroom Advanced

Skin Relief Face Serum.

If this wasn't the height of barefaced cheek I don't know what is. I would have thought that a nationally respected company such as Boots would discourage such blatant opportunism in their sales staff.

Sincerely

T Ravenscroft (Mr)

**Customer Care**
**PO Box 5300**
**Nottingham**
**NG90 1AA**

CS/14482509
16 January 2015

Mr T Ravenscroft
19 Victoria Gardens
New Mills
High Peak
SK12 4BC

Dear Mr Ravenscroft

Thank you for contacting us about your recent visit to one of our stores.

I understand you were disappointed to find that Boots do not offer a Mushroom Testing/identifying service and I appreciate you letting us know how you feel.

I have taken this opportunity to send our Pharmacy Service Team a copy of your letter. They have reassured me your comments will be raised and considered at their next review.

I was sorry to learn that when you enquired about this service at your local store, our assistant was uninterested and tried to sell you a bottle of Mega Mushroom Advanced Skin Relief Serum.

This clearly is not the standard of service we aim to provide. I would like the chance to feed this back to the Store Manager. For me to do so, please could you let me know which of our stores this happened in?

Yours sincerely

Vanessa Brazener
Customer Care

19 Victoria Gardens
New Mills
High Peak
SK12 4BC

22nd January 2014

Vanessa Brazener
Boots Customer Care
PO Box 5300
Nottingham
NG90 1AA

Dear Vanessa Brazener

Reference your assistant who tried to sell me a bottle of Mega Mushroom Advanced Skin Relief and your request for further information.

I am a gentleman, and as such would not dream of getting a young lady in trouble. Apart from that I suspect she was not a regular assistant on the counter at which Mega Mushroom Advanced Skin Relief may be purchased, but in all likelihood, judging from the amount of make-up trowelled on her face, was a fugitive from one of the numerous cosmetics counters, and was just standing in for the day.

I hope that your Pharmacy Services Team will soon have a mushroom testing facility up and running. However I am not holding my breath.

Incidentally, I get my medications from a pharmacy outlet of yours attached to the local Medical Centre. Prominently displayed on the wall by the counter is a notice that reads: 'Today's Responsible Pharmacist is….' followed by the name of the pharmacist. Why is this? Do you have an Irresponsible Pharmacist too? If you do it might be a good opening for the counter assistant who tried to sell me the Mega Mushroom Advanced Skin Relief.

Sincerely

T Ravenscroft (Mr)

## NO REPLY!

****

19 Victoria Gardens
New Mills
High Peak
SK12 4BC

11th February 2015

Dairyfoods For You
2 Harbinson Road
Leicester
LE8 4BK

Dear Dairyfoods For You

I am the secretary of the recently formed self-help group Deprived Residents on Social Security (DROSS). Our manifesto is to help ourselves and others who unfortunately find themselves having to survive on state social security payments, with all the hardship that entails. One of the group's aims is to try to come up with ideas for meals that provide adequate sustenance, whilst at the same time being inexpensive to produce. One such meal, created by our Mr Stansfield, who has experience in the kitchens of our nearby Stepping Hill Hospital, is our Offal and Beans Bake, (which tastes a lot nicer than it sounds.) I won't take up your time by listing all the ingredients of the dish, but the main ones, the indispensible ones, are tripe (black, honeycomb, or a mixture of the two), Big Bean Company beans and Dairyfoods For You Garlic Mayonnaise.

It is the Dairyfoods For You Garlic Mayonnaise that is the cause of the problem; for whilst the offal and beans are fairly cheap to acquire - we have an arrangement with a local slaughterhouse for the offal and the Big Beans Company's beans are one of the cheaper brands - the Dairyfoods

For You Garlic Mayonnaise is comparatively expensive. We have tried adding garlic to other brands of mayonnaise, Hellmans etc, and to a garlic salad cream, but the dish just isn't the same. In fact the salad cream made the dish look most unpalatable, its yellow colour tending to turn the offal and bean mix an unattractive khaki colour (unattractive, that is, except to our World War 2 veteran Mr Havery, who said it reminded him of his great time in the army) which of course creamy white mayonnaise doesn't.

Bearing the above in mind I was wondering if you do a less expensive version of your garlic mayonnaise that we might substitute?

Sincerely

T Ravenscroft (Mr)

Hon Sec DROSS

DAIRYFOODS FOR YOU

Ref: 44439
18 February 2015

T Ravenscroft
19 Victoria Gardens
New Mills
High Peak
SK12 4BC

Dear Mr Ravenscroft

Thank you for your letter of 21 Feb. It is always nice to hear from satisfied customers.

I am afraid we do not provide a less expensive version of our Dairyfoods For You

Garlic Mayonnaise. However can I offer a suggestion? Between you and me our Dairyfoods For You Mayonnaise is exactly the same recipe as our Dairyfoods For You Garlic Mayonnaise, excepting that the garlic has been left out. And it is *28 pence cheaper* for the same size jar. So how would it be if you bought our Dairyfoods For You Mayonnaise and added your own garlic, thus saving you 28 pence per jar, less the cost of the garlic?

I enclose a £3 voucher for our Dairyfoods For You Mayonnaise so that you can try this out. Good luck.

Yours sincerely
Daphne Winterston, Customer Care.

**Dairyfoods For You, 2 Harbinson Road, Leicester, LE8 4BK**

*

19 Victoria Gardens
New Mills
High Peak
SK12 4BC

27th February 2015

Dairyfoods For You
2 Harbinson Road
Leicester
LE8 4BK

Dear Daphne

What an excellent suggestion! God bless you! We implemented it immediately. So that others might also benefit from it I put it on my facebook page (4572 friends), my twitter page ( 3908 followers) , and DROSS's facebook page (5921 friends) and twitter page (1896 followers) that your Dairyfoods For You Garlic Mayonnaise is 28 pence dearer than your Dairyfoods For You Mayonnaise, despite the only difference being that it has about 2 penceworth (approx) of garlic in it. I have also asked our facebook friends to share this information and for our twitter friends to re-tweet it. It could very well go viral. Let's hope so. Of course the downside is that Dairyfoods For You will be short of 26 pence multiplied by however many jars of Dairyfoods For You Garlic Mayonnaise you used to sell, but what is that compared to the feeling of satisfaction you must have had in making it possible for us to make our Offal and Beans Bake cheaper?

Thank you again

Sincerely

T Ravenscroft (Mr)

****

19 Victoria Gardens
New Mills
High Peak
SK12 4BC

2nd January 2015

Waitrose Ltd
Doncastle Road
Bracknell
RG12 8YA

Dear Waitrose

While my wife was visiting her sister for a few days I thought I would depart from her usual choice in the soup line - a selection from the prosaic food manufacturer Heinz, or Asda Smartprice Tomato - and treat myself to some of your superior Alvalle Original Gazpacho. While the cat is away the mice will play, I suppose you might say. Well if that is the case what we have now is a very sick mouse, for to say that I found your soup disappointing is a bit like saying that the Archduke Franz Ferdinand was a bit pissed off the day that Bosnian Serb fellow shot him. Indeed I would have expected a soup that cost 41p per 100ml to be something special, when in truth it wasn't as good as Heinz Classic Vegetable Soup, at 22p per 100ml, with which I compared it. Admittedly the Heinz soup contains carrots, potatoes and peas, all of which the gazpacho eschews in favour of cucumber, but even allowing for the additional flavour imparted by the carrots etc your soup does not even begin compare in quality, at least not where my taste buds are concerned - and I speak as a man whose taste sensations are sufficiently educated to have advised him in the past that he will not be best pleased on dining at Burger King.

Suffice to say I will not be buying any more of your soups.

Sincerely

T Ravenscroft (Mr)

Waitrose

Mr T Ravenscroft
19 Victoria Gardens
New Mills
High Peak
SK12 4BC

15 January 2015

1-162891079-7

Dear Mr Ravenscroft

Thanks for letting us know that one of our products you purchased from Ocado was not of the standard you expected. I'm very sorry this happened and thought it would be helpful for you to know what we'll do with the information. The details you provided have been passed to our merchants complaints department to investigate. We're keen to achieve the very highest standards of quality in the products we sell and work hard to make sure these are maintained.

Our buyers and technologists work closely with our producers and suppliers to alert them to any concerns. Unfortunately, it does appear that something went wrong on this occasion, but I hope you'll be reassured to know that the information you've given us will help us stop this from happening again.

In view of what's happened I enclose vouchers

which can be used at any branch of Waitrose or John Lewis. I hope we'll see you again soon.

Yours sincerely

Lauren Baker
**Section Manager, Customer Service**
Enclosed Vouchers £9.00

**Customer Service, Bracknell, Berkshire, RG12 8YA**

19 Victoria Gardens
New Mills
High Peak
SK12 4BC

22nd January 2015

Lauren Baker
Waitrose Ltd
Doncastle Road
Bracknell
RG12 8YA

Your ref: 1-162891079-7

Dear Lauren Baker

Do I feel foolish! I didn't know that Alvalle Original Gazpacho was meant to be eaten cold! Who would have thought it? *Cold* Soup? My wife informed me of this astounding (to me) fact on her return from her sisters when I mentioned my disappointment with it. (But of course by that time I had already written to you complaining about it.)

Thank you for the vouchers totalling £9.00. I wasn't at all surprised by your generosity - if your partner John Lewis can afford to fork out a £1,000,000 every year for its Christmas TV commercial you must be minting it between the two of you, and therefore well able to afford it.

I spent £4.10 of the money on another carton of Alvalle Original Gazpacho; and this time I ate it as it is supposed to be eaten, cold. I must be honest with you; it tasted worse cold than it did hot. So I gave up the ghost and with the balance bought 8 cans of Heinz Vegetable. Much more palatable, hot *or* cold.

None of my business of course, but might it not be to the advantage of all concerned if instead of handing out with gay abandon vouchers to the value of £9 you invested the money in improving the quality of your Alvalle Original Gazpacho?

Sincerely

T Ravenscroft (Mr)

****

19 Victoria Gardens
New Mills
High Peak
SK12 4BC

9th December 2014

Kezie Ltd
Burnhouses Farm
Duns
Berwickshire
TD11 3TT

Dear Kezie

Since first trying your camel meat last year I have dined on it, either in the form of a cut of steak or as the main ingredient of a casserole, at least once a fortnight, and have found it to be as excellent a red meat as money can buy. The only trouble is that I have started to grow a hump. No I haven't, that's just a joke, a reminder to myself that I have a sense of humour.

A sense of humour is certainly something I needed a couple of years ago when on holiday in Lanzarote I rode up Fire Mountain on a camel. I have heard of camels referred to as 'Ships of the Desert'. My camel was the shit of the desert, and proved it within seconds of our setting off when it took it upon itself to throw a fit, which resulted in my being unceremoniously deposited on the rocky ground and sustaining a broken leg in two places; one where I fell off the camel, and another five yards back down the mountain when I rolled into a boulder. It completely ruined my holiday of course, so you may well understand why I have harboured a desire to get my own back on the beasts ever since. When I saw your advert for camel meat I realised that eating camel would be one way of doing it. That camel meat tastes very nice is a bonus, and has made my revenge all the sweeter.

I am by no means a vindictive man, much less macabre, but it dawned on me recently that my revenge would be even sweeter if I could actually see the camels that I will one day be eating. To this end I was wondering if you at Kezie have a visitor centre and perhaps do conducted tours of your farm?

Sincerely

T Ravenscroft (Mr)

**Kezie**
always adventurous with food

**Burnhouses Farm**
**Duns**
**Berwickshire**
**TD11 3TT**

27th January 2015

19 Victoria Gardens
New Mills
High Peak
SK12 4BC

Dear Mr Ravenscroft,

First of all, thank you for your correspondence.

Customers like yourself, who have a true passion and calling in their life, are one of the main reasons we love doing what we do. Your sheer enthusiasm for the consumption of 'Land Ships' is one of the most inspiring stories I have personally read in the past decade.

Your joke about growing a hump was most humorous, and reading it out in the office prompted some well received sighs, groans and I believe a snort.

I am sorry to hear of your harrowing tale in the far away land of Lanzarote. You must have felt like a real-life Captain Ahab whilst wrestling with such a ferocious beast. Hopefully your leg has suffered no lasting ill-effects (although a cool Camel related scar must be a hit with the ladies?)

As for your request, unfortunately all our Camels are located in Australia. Due to time zone issues I think even a Skype call might be out of the question.

Best wishes on your eating adventures,

The Kezie Team

19 Victoria Gardens
New Mills
High Peak
SK12 4BC

4th February 2015

Kezie Ltd
Burnhouses Farm
Duns
Berwickshire
TD11 3TT

Dear Kezie Team

Thank you for your reply. A little flippant maybe, but perhaps excusable given the circumstances.

Having perused your price list more objectively I now see that what happened to me on the Lanzarote camel was in all probability an act of retribution by the camel - a case of the beast taking its revenge on the human race for your charging the exorbitant price of £16.76 for a 250g pack of fillet of its Australian cousins. No wonder it was upset and acted as it did.

Sincerely

T Ravenscroft (Mr)

****

19 Victoria Gardens
New Mills
High Peak
SK12 4BC

7th January 2015

Ann Summers
Godstone Road
Whyteleafe
Surrey
CR3 0GG

Dear Ann Summers

I wonder if you could help me? Recently, whilst looking in the drawer of the bedside cabinet on my wife's side of the bed to see if my gold cuff links had inadvertently found their way in there, I came across a packet of your BJ Mints. Now I am a man of the world, well aware of the Ann Summers shops and the sort of things in which they trade, so it came as something of a surprise that you also sold confectionary. What didn't come as a surprise was that the mints were penis-shaped - indeed I wouldn't expect anything else from a company who sold sex aids; in fact I found the idea quite amusing.

A thing that intrigued me though, and is the cause of my writing to you, is the name of the mint. Why BJ? What do the initials stand for? I racked my brains; Blueberry Juice, perhaps? Blackcurrant Joys? Breathtakingly Jaunty? Nothing I could think of seemed to make much sense. So I give in; what is it?
Sincerely

T Ravenscroft (Mr)

Ann Summers

Mr Ravenscroft
19 Victoria Gardens
New Mills
High Peak
SK12 4BC

4th February 2015

Dear Mr Ravenscroft

I am contacting you regarding your recent communication to Ann Summers. I would like to confirm the 'BJ' on our 'BJ Mints' stands for the act of fellatio (Blow Job). They are sucked after giving head to take the taste of semen away.

I hope this clarifies the name of our product and if you have any further questions or queries, please do not hesitate to contact us.

Kind Regards,

Sarah Ferguson
Customer Services Advisor

19 Victoria Gardens
New Mills
High Peak
SK12 4BC

7th January 2015

Sarah Ferguson
Ann Summers
Godstone Road
Whyteleafe
Surrey
CR3 0GG

Dear Sarah Ferguson

First of all please allow me to commiserate with you on having reached such a low point in your life that you have to work in the sex industry to earn a crust. For my money your ex, Prince Andrew, is twice the philanderer you ever were (and is proving the point even as I write). Better luck in the future with your men!

As far as the BJ Mints and your explanation of their function is concerned I can only think that my wife must have made an error, perhaps mistaking them for some other sweet, because she hasn't given me a blow job within living memory.

Which begs the question…?

Yours sincerely

T Ravenscroft (Mr)

****

19 Victoria Gardens
New Mills
High Peak
SK12 4BC
23rd January 2015

Denhay Farms Ltd
Devonshire Road
Honiton
EX14 1SD

Dear Denhay Farms

For reasons I won't bother you with I have recently been forced to take over my family's food shopping/cooking duties. This has led to me having to make a complaint about your bacon. My wife has always purchased our bacon from the local Sainsbury's; yet the bacon I purchased from there yesterday, yours, is nothing like the bacon to which I have become accustomed. For one thing it doesn't taste the same. If I were to hazard a guess I would say that it could be because, unlike our usual bacon, your bacon ends up the same size after cooking it as it started out; which suggests to me that it isn't frying properly, and therefore is not cooked sufficiently. In addition to not shrinking to about half its original size your bacon also retains the same shape throughout its spell in the frying pan and, again unlike our usual bacon, doesn't crinkle up into a sort of corrugated shape. Finally, it doesn't shed any little globules of white stuff - obviously an important part of the cooking process - which could be a further reason why it doesn't taste the same as the bacon I am used to. Could your bacon's refusal to fry correctly be because of something untoward you have done to it during the manufacturing process? I didn't eat it of course; I am well aware of the havoc that eating insufficiently cooked food can do to one's system, having once fallen foul of a doner kebab.

I would appreciate your observations.

Sincerely

T Ravenscroft (Mr)

DENHAY

Mr T Ravenscroft
19 Victoria Gardens
New Mills
High Peak
SK12 4B

**29 January 20.**

**Ref: Denhay Dry Cured Bacon.**

Dear Mr Ravenscroft

We were sorry you were disappointed with a recent purchase of Denhay Dry Cure Bacon. We have never received a complaint like yours before and we were rather perplexed by your comments about our bacon.

The comments you have made in your letter suggests that you have more experience of some of the other brands that are available at Sainsbury's. Typically these are bacon products that have been produced using a method of injecting brine into the pork to enable rapid maturation. This is followed by a freezing step to produce a more uniform product and to facilitate the slicing process. The consequences of this modern process of bacon manufacture are that during cooking, the rashers will often release 'white stuff', shrink and crinkle up as you have described in your letter.

We would like to reassure you that Denhay Dry

Cure Bacon is a top quality, traditionally produced dry cured bacon product. By this we mean that we hand massage a sea salt mixture onto each British pork loin or belly and allow it to mature slowly to develop a fuller flavour. Our traditional method does not use freezing as part of the process and we pride ourselves that our bacon exhibits the natural variation associated with a quality pork product.

Many thanks for taking the trouble to contact us, as comments such as yours are very valuable to us.

Yours sincerely

Wendy Williams
Quality Manager

**Denhay Farms, Devonshire Rd, Heathpark, Honiton, EX14 1SD**

19 Victoria Gardens
New Mills
High Peak
SK12 4BC
4th February 2015

Wendy Williams
Denhay Farms Ltd
Devonshire Road
Honiton
EX14 1SD

Dear Wendy Williams

It doesn't surprise me at all that you have never received a complaint like mine before. The English as a race are loath to complain; fortunately the small amount of Scottish blood in me adds a little grumpiness to my otherwise benevolent nature.

Thank you for the information about your bacon. You were so enthusiastic about it I was inspired to give you another chance, and purchased another packet. I then blind-tasted it against the usual bacon we get from Sainsbury's, frying the two bacons in separate frying pans to avoid any cross contamination. I must report that I much preferred our usual bacon. I gave up on yours after a couple of mouthfuls, finding it far too 'chewy'. I gave the rest to the cat, which ate it, but without showing much enthusiasm.

Could I offer a suggestion? Perhaps you should consider including in your process those things which you criticize other bacon producers for - injection of brine and freezing - which, along with a less liberal use of sea salt, might encourage your bacon to shrivel, crinkle and emit white stuff, a process that quite obviously improves the taste.

There is also the question of my wasting £3.15 on buying another 200g of your bacon, thanks to your going over the top about its merits. You might feel that you should compensate me for this (although not with a voucher for more of your bacon, please).

Sincerely

T Ravenscroft (Mr)

## NO REPLY!

****

19 Victoria Gardens
New Mills
High Peak
SK12 4BC

January 2nd 2015

Lockwoods
Ripley Road
Belper
Derbyshire
DE56 2JR

Dear Lockwoods

My wife had bought not nearly enough guacamole for the buffet we were putting on to celebrate our wedding anniversary, and there wasn't time to get any more. I then had the idea of making it spin out with a bag of your Lockwoods Mushy Peas, guacamole being approximately the same consistency and colour of mushy peas. My wife pooh-poohed the idea, and remarked that just because sticky toffee pudding and poo were the same consistency and colour it didn't mean that sticky toffee pudding would still taste like sticky toffee pudding if you were to mix the two together; however she was possibly upset because I'd ticked her off for not buying enough guacamole in the first place. (Not being a fan of sticky toffee pudding I might have mentioned that *anything* mixed in with it could only improve it, but I didn't want to risk upsetting her further.)

Anyway, I went ahead with the plan, using equal quantities of guacamole and mushy peas. I can report that not only did no one at the party notice the difference but that several of them said it was the best guacamole they had ever tasted! It could only have been the addition of the mushy peas that brought about this reaction as we've served up Sainsbury's own brand guacamole many times in the past without it ever eliciting favourable comments; indeed on a couple of occasions it has been the cause of a disappointed wrinkling of noses. Two of the people who praised it, one of whom was local radio Dave Diamond (not his real name), asked me for the recipe. When I told them it was nothing more than Sainsbury's bog standard guacamole mixed with an equal proportion of your mushy peas they wouldn't believe me. However I did eventually manage to convince them.

The thing is, Dave Diamond, who includes a home entertaining spot on his show every Thursday, asked me if I would mind if he gave out the recipe on his show. Well I don't mind; the thing is, do you mind? Dave says that along with the recipe he would give your excellent product a name check. Can I therefore pass on to him your permission?

Sincerely

T Ravenscroft (Mr)

Lockwood
THE HOME OF MUSHY PEAS

Mr T Ravenscroft
19 Victoria Gardens
New Mills
High Peak
SK12 4BC

29 January 2015

Dear Mr Ravenscroft

Thank you so much for taking the trouble to write to us.

Isn't it really interesting that some great ideas happen as a result of having a problem to solve? I'm glad that you didn't listen to your wife on this occasion, and delighted that the buffet was a success.

We are upgrading our website at the minute, and funnily enough, we plan to put a guacamole recipe on it. We would be delighted if Dave Diamond shared the recipe on his show - I can't think of a better way of spreading the word.

I hope that you continue to enjoy our peas.

Anne Thornhill

General Manager
Lockwoods Ltd

**Lockwoods, Ripley Road, Ambergate, Derbyshire, DE56 2JR**

19 Victoria Gardens
New Mills
High Peak
SK12 4BC

February 5th 2015

Anne Thornhill
Lockwoods
Ripley Road
Belper
Derbyshire
DE56 2JR

Dear Anne Thornhill

So you at Lockwoods are to introduce a recipe for guacamole on your website? What a coincidence! A more suspicious man than I might think that you stole the idea from me. Dave Diamond did, and, a more mercenary individual than I, said that I should take you to the cleaners. However, you have my word as a Ravenscroft that I would never do such an underhand thing.

Dave asked me to thank you and says he will ‘give your mushies a mensh’ (his way of saying he will refer to your product) on his show. He also points out that as a local DJ he isn’t paid much, and that a small fee for this favour - even a payment in kind - would be much appreciated. In exchange he is prepared to mention Lockwoods Mushy Peas, their use as a guacamole ingredient, and your new website, every week for six months. I suggest that perhaps a fiver or a dozen cans of mushy peas would keep him happy.

Please let me know if I can pass on to him news

of your agreement to such an arrangement.

Sincerely

T Ravenscroft (Mr)

NO REPLY!

****

19 Victoria Gardens
New Mills
High Peak
SK12 4BC

2nd January 2015

Tesco Customer Services
PO Box 73
Dundee
DD1 9NF

Dear Sir

I recently purchased a packet of your Tesco Ken Hom Spare Ribs. There was a picture of a fat Chinese gentleman on the front of the packet and if it is a facsimile of Ken Hom he certainly didn't get fat by eating his brand of spare ribs. Being generous I would estimate that the ratio of bone to meat was about 15 to 1 in favour of bone. Indeed if a jockey were to use the whip on his horse more than a couple of times it would end up with more meat on it.

To spend the time I should have spent eating meat I counted the list of ingredients on the back of the packet. There were twenty seven, so maybe there wasn't room left for much meat. If that is the case might I suggest that you leave out a few of them, possibly the Orange Juice from Concentrate, and the Molasses, both of which I think I could forfeit without it breaking my heart.

Anyway you live and learn; and, as the kamikaze pilot said as he went out on his first mission, 'Never again.'

Yours sincerely

T Ravenscroft (Mr)

TESCO
*Every little helps*

**Tesco Customer Services**
**PO Box 73**
**Dundee**
**DD1 9NF**

10th January 2015

Mr T Ravenscroft
19 Victoria Gardens
New Mills
High Peak
SK12 4BC

Dear Mr Ravenscroft

Thank you for your recent letter. I'm very sorry that your Ken Hom Spare Ribs hardly had any meat on them. I can understand how annoying this must have been for you, especially as you must have been looking forward to eating them.

We work hard, together with our suppliers, to maintain the highest standards of our meat. Our suppliers run quality assurance checks throughout the production process, to make sure that the best cuts make it into our stores. Our Technical Managers make regular visits to our suppliers to make sure they are meeting our strict quality standards.

Normally, I'd ask our supplier to look into you complaint, but unfortunately without the packaging information, I'm unable to do so. The packaging allows us to identify the right product and supplier, as well as the batch it came from.

If you still have the packaging, or find a fault with any product in future, please take it to your local store with a sample of the product if you have one. Our staff will then complete a customer complaint form, which allows us to look into this further for you. Alternatively, you can send the packaging to me at the above address.

However, to say sorry, I've enclosed a £10.00 Tesco Moneycard for you with my apologies. It's yours to spend how you please and I hope you can buy yourself something nice with this.

Thanks for telling us about this. After all, we'd much rather know if something's wrong, so we can put it right as soon as possible.

Yours sincerely
For and on behalf of Tesco Stores Ltd

Joanne De-Souza
Customer Service Manager

Enc: £10.00 Tesco Moneycard

19 Victoria Gardens
New Mills
High Peak
SK12 4BC

17th January 2015

Joanne De-Souza
Tesco Customer Services
PO Box 73
Dundee
DD1 9NF

Dear Joanne De-Souza

Thank you for your reply. Welcome as it was I am afraid I must pick you up on a couple of points.

Firstly, your contention that without the packaging that would allow you to identify the right product and supplier you are unable to look into my complaint. Well the item in question is called Tesco Ken Hom Spare Ribs, which clearly identifies the product, (Ken Hom Spare Ribs), and the supplier, (Tesco). Just how much identification do you need?

Secondly, you said that the Tesco Moneycard you sent was mine to spend how I pleased and that you hoped I could buy something nice with it. This just isn't true, because I tried to spend it at Marks and Spencers on a nice pair of tartan boxer shorts that had recently taken my eye and they refused to accept it; indeed they got quite snotty about it when I showed them your letter.

In fact they did me a favour because soon afterwards I had an idea that put it to far better use. Unbelievably - in view of my opinion of your

Ken Hom Spare Ribs - I bought another four packets of the stuff. There was, however, method in my apparent madness. A few weeks ago I had one of the worst dining experiences I have ever had in my life - and I speak as a man who has been exposed to hospital food and Kentucky Fried Chicken - when my wife and I were invited for a meal at the home of a couple I had until then thought of as friends. The main course was a truly revolting lasagne. The lady of the house claimed it was home-made, but, suspecting she was lying, whilst I was alone in the kitchen I had a quick look in her waste bin and inside, sure enough, was a supermarket lasagne packet. You will be glad to learn that it wasn't Tesco's, although you shouldn't get too pleased about this as I once risked one of yours and it was almost as bad.

Anyway, as we hadn't yet returned the dinner invitation - in fact we weren't going to, in the hope that if we didn't invite them they wouldn't invite us again and maybe finish us off altogether with a supermarket moussaka - we went ahead and invited them. For what better way was there to get our own back than by serving up a portion of Tesco Ken Hom Spare Ribs? Fortunately, or unfortunately if you were depending on them for sustenance, they were as lacking in meat as the ones I made the complaint about. You could see from the expression on the faces of our guests that they weren't best pleased. In fact in an unguarded moment I overheard one of them say that it was the last time they'd ever be coming; which suited me just fine.

The thing is I spent all the £10 Tesco Moneycard

on the Ken Hom Spare Ribs, so I didn't really get the chance to buy myself something nice with it, and I was wondering if you could send me another one?

Yours sincerely

T Ravenscroft (Mr)

TESCO
Every little helps

**Tesco Customer Services**
**PO Box 73**
**Dundee**
**DD1 9NF**

27 January 2015

Mr T Ravenscroft
19 Victoria Gardens
New Mills
High Peak
SK12 4BC

Dear Mr Ravenscroft

Thank you for your letter of reply on 28 May. I apologise you were unhappy with my response with regards to our Ken Hom Spare Ribs. I understand you must have been a little disappointed because there was no packaging we were unable to do a full investigation.

I'm sorry to hear your dinner party at your friend's house was not very successful and you were hoping you would not be invited back but you were. So you invited them to yours and decided to give our Hen Hobs Spare Ribs (sic) another go at your dinner party. Unfortunately, these were no better than the ones you had before.

As you had another disappointing experience with these Spare Ribs I've called our supplier again and noted on the first complaint we sent to them that you have bought these again and once again they were disappointing. I've now enclosed a further £10.00 Moneycard for you with my best wishes and I hope you buy something nice for yourself this time. If I can help with anything else please let me know. Thanks for taking the time and trouble to contact us.

Yours sincerely
For and on behalf of Tesco Stores Ltd

Joanne De-Souza
Customer Service Manager

Enc: £10.00 Tesco Moneycard

19 Victoria Gardens
New Mills
High Peak
SK12 4BC

30th January 2015

Bernard Matthews Ltd
Great Witchingham Hall
Norwich
NR9 5QD

Dear Bernard Matthews

My wife recently purchased a packet of your Wafer Thin Turkey Ham. I always make a point of checking out the ingredients of any product new to me ever since I discovered that there was no butter in Utterly Butterly, and that the seafood in Young's Seafood Sticks was notable by its absence, so on taking this precaution I wasn't totally surprised to find no mention of ham on your packet. How can this be? In a product calling itself Turkey Ham - and whilst by no means expecting fifty per cent of turkey and fifty per cent of ham, the latter of course being more expensive and therefore not as attractive to you - I would expect to find a least *some* ham, even if it were just enough ham to keep you honest.

Can you please explain this non-appearance of ham in your Turkey Ham?

Sincerely

T Ravenscroft (Mr)

Bernard Matthews

2nd February 2015

Mr T Ravenscroft
19 Victoria Gardens
New Mills
High Peak
SK12 4BC

Dear Mr Ravenscroft

Thank you for your letter received on 2nd February regarding out Wafer Thin Turkey Ham. We are sorry that it was necessary for you to contact us and we are pleased to be given the opportunity to resolve the matter.

Although the word ham is usually associated with pork there is also a tradition around the world of curing meat from other animals and birds and referring to it as 'ham'. The word ham refers to the thigh muscle and if you are a sports-person you are no doubt very familiar with the expression 'ham-strings'.

Our turkey ham is made using the full-flavoured thigh and drumstick meat from our own British farmed turkeys. The meat is carefully trimmed from the bone by our trained butchers before it is prepared for curing and being made up into the familiar family favourite that has proved popular over the last 20 years.

As we trust you will appreciate, the term 'turkey ham' is used to identify the product only. We then use a full product designation on the pack to fully describe the product to show what it is made of, as below:-

Turkey Ham: - reformed from cured turkey with added water, starch and milk protein.

We hope the above information is of some help to you. We have pleasure in enclosing our voucher for £3.00 for you to purchase a product of your choice.

Thank you for taking the time to contact us.

Yours sincerely,
For BERNARD MATTHEWS FARMS LTD

Emma Wilson
CUSTOMER INFORMATION ADMINISTRATOR

**Bernard Matthews Ltd, Great Witchingham Hall, Norwich, NR9 5QD**

19 Victoria Gardens
New Mills
High Peak
SK12 4BC

5th February 2015

Emma Wilson
Bernard Matthews Ltd
Great Witchingham Hall
Norwich
NR9 5QD

Dear Emma Wilson

Thank you for the excuse you gave for calling your product Turkey Ham.

Unfortunately my eyes aren't as good as they were - a problem shared with many of your older customers I would guess - and therefore the very small print on your full product designation - reformed cured turkey with added water, starch and milk protein - might just as well say it is made from the dried intestines of the Australian Bush Whippet with added bat droppings.

With the above in mind, in the interests of transparency, and perhaps as a way to avoid duping the general public into buying something other than what they think they are buying, would it not be better to call your product Wafer Thin Reformed Turkey Drumstick, Water, Starch and Milk Protein? Or do you think your sales might suffer were you to do this?

Sincerely

T Ravenscroft (Mr)

NO REPLY!

****

19 Victoria Gardens
New Mills
High Peak
SK12 4BC

5th January 2015

The Dalmore Distillery
Alness
Ross-shire
Scotland
IV17 0UT

Dear Dalmore Distillery

I recently took one of your Distillery Tours. Unfortunately what should have been a pleasant and rewarding experience was completely spoiled for me by another person taking the tour. This man, obviously an individual who is in love with the sound of his own voice, continually interrupted your tour guide with questions he obviously knew the answers to, no doubt because he'd been on similar tours before. 'Is it true that whilst the Golden Promise variety of barley has been popular for many years, these days distillers use alternatives like Optic and Chariot as well?' was one of his queries. Another was, as near as I can remember, 'Is it a fact that after the hot water has been added to the grist, the liquid drained off as a result is called the wort?' Believe me when I say that it took all my patience to refrain from hurling him bodily into one of your large vats (of which he enquired of your guide if it was true that they were traditionally known as mash tuns. *As if he didn't know!*)

In order that your future tours aren't spoiled in a

similar manner for others might I suggest that the placing of suitable notices displayed in prominent places throughout the tour might be appropriate? Something like ‘Please reserve your questions until the tour is over’, or, perhaps a little more succinctly, if not discreetly, ‘Will smartarses kindly keep their cakeholes shut during the tour’.

Sincerely

T Ravenscroft (Mr)

THE DALMORE

28 January 2015

19 Victoria Gardens
New Mills
High Peak
SK12 4BC

Dear Mr Ravenscroft

Thank you for your letter dated 24th January.

I am sorry to hear that your tour was spoiled by another visitor on that day, believe me it is a constant problem that is shared by all other distilleries that I am in contact with.

Some of our visitors are doing so for the first time and their knowledge of the process is limited. Others are whisky enthusiasts and try and 'bag' as many distillery tours as possible during their stay in Scotland, and then we have the visitor who likes to impart his knowledge to the rest of the group.

Our guides are trained to deal with this situation as politely and sensitively as possible but occasionally we do host guests who test us. Sadly, we have no way of knowing how the tour will go before we leave and can only try and pace the tour to the level of the group in front of us.

I take on board your suggestion on signage and that is something I will look into. In the meantime, I would like to offer you and your guests a private tour if you are in the area again and a couple of drams on me.

Thank you for choosing to visit The Dalmore and I sincerely hope we can put right this wrong and deliver a more rewarding experience in the future.

Kind regards,

**SHAUNA JENNENS**
**Dalmore Distillery Ambassador**

**The Dalmore Distillery, Alness, Ross-shire, Scotland, IV17 0UT**

19 Victoria Gardens
New Mills
High Peak
SK12 4BC

5th February 2015

Shauna Jennens
The Dalmore Distillery
Alness
Ross-shire
Scotland
IV17 0UT

Dear Shauna Jennens

Thank you for your letter and the invitations of a private tour and a couple of drams. It gives me great pleasure in taking you up on your kind offer. My wife and I will be touring in The Highlands again during the week April 12 to 18, so any date within those limits would be capital. We can arrange our itinerary to fit in with this.

Getting back to my original reason for writing to you, might I offer a further suggestion, in addition to suitable signage, that may help weed out potential tour spoilers?

1. Bar anyone Scottish. Scottish people, without exception, know all about whisky, therefore their being on the tour can only be for 'imparting their knowledge' reasons.

2. Bar anyone from Australia. They are obviously only there for the free whisky at the end of the tour. If that wasn't enough, anything they say will not make a scrap of

sense and would only contribute to spoiling it for the rest of the visitors.

3. Bar anyone Japanese. Or at the very least confiscate their cameras for the duration of their visit. The Japanese photograph anything and everything. This inevitably slows down the tour, to the annoyance of others. On the tour I took one man photographed his wife every time we stopped, then she photographed him, then they asked someone to take a photo of the two of them together. Every time this happened the tour was delayed until they had finished. My only consolation is that when they asked me to photograph them I only pretended to - so they won't now have a photo of them grinning manically in front of your iconic royal stag's antlers, along with their other snaps. It was either that or hang them from the stag's antlers.

4. Bar anyone German. As far as I know Germans don't share any of the annoying tendencies that Scots, Australians and Japanese exhibit when visiting distilleries, but that doesn't mean to say they won't exhibit them in the future. Germans are not to be trusted. Two World Wars. Angela Merkel. Lidl and Aldi. Enough said.

Sincerely

T Ravenscroft (Mr)

****

19 Victoria Gardens
New Mills
High Peak
SK12 4BC

7th February 2015

Belmond Le Manoir aux Quat'Saisons
Church Road
Great Milton
Oxford
OX44 7PD

Dear Belmond

A devoted gourmet and keen amateur chef, a huge fan of Raymond Blanc, a Francophile, I am toying with the idea of enlisting on one of your Maman Blanc one-day cookery courses. (A neighbour took one of Raymond's courses a few years ago with excellent results.) Before I commit to it however, and to assure myself that I will benefit from the experience, I would like to know if *Le Patron* uses an interpreter whilst he is teaching his class to cook. I require this information because, although I bow to no one in my admiration of Monsieur Blanc's culinary expertise, and watch all his TV programmes avidly, I can't for the life of me tell me what the hell he is talking about. This doesn't bother me when he is on TV - I simply switch on the subtitles - but there won't be any subtitles in his kitchen when he's making with the pots and pans and I would probably end up utterly frustrated and knowing less about cooking than I did before the lesson started, which is the last thing I want at £385 a pop.

So if you can please advise me? Should Raymond not use the services of an interpreter during his lessons my good friend Mr Atkins, who is fluent in French, has agreed to accompany me, as long as he wouldn't be expected to pay. (Unlike me he has no interest in cooking.)

Sincerely

T Ravenscroft (Mr)

## NO REPLY!

****

19 Victoria Gardens
New Mills
High Peak
SK12 4BC

3rd January 2015

Customer Services
Pataks Foods Ltd
Kiribati Way
Leigh
Lancashire
WN7 5RS

Dear Pataks

*"I love the fact that what we eat in our home you can now eat in yours. Whether it's sauces, or pastes, or pickles or pappadums they're all authentically Indian and many use our own secret blends of spices that no-one outside the family knows!"*

*Anjali Patak*

I remembered the above quote, although not the exact wording, when I had cause to stay overnight in Leigh last week. If I'm not mistaken I read it on one of your jars of curry paste; it is certainly on your website because I looked it up the following day to make sure I got it right.

To pass the evening in Leigh I spent a couple of hours in one of the local pubs, the Boars Head. Whilst standing at the saloon bar enjoying a pint I overheard a man ask an Indian - who obviously worked at Patak's factory - if it was really true that no one outside the Patak family knew the secret blends of spices used in their curries; or was it perhaps just something the Patak family wish people to believe in order to create a good impression. The Indian said it was a load of rubbish, and backed this up by saying that only the other day he had witnessed one of his fellow operatives running out of the relevant spice mix when making a batch of Rogan Josh sauce, whereupon the foreman told him to 'bung in a similar amount of Korma spice mix and a bit more chilli.' The Indian went on to say that it wasn't the first time this sort of thing had happened - he himself had once been urged to double the amount of cinnamon when he ran out of allspice - and that in his opinion Patak's curry sauces were about as authentically Indian as Ben Kingsley was in Gandhi. Quite obviously then, if indeed your spice blends are secret, it is a secret not so dear to your heart that you aren't prepared to put it to one side when it is expedient to do so. I suppose you could argue that the combination of Rogan Josh and Korma spices and a bit more chilli is another of your secrets, but that's hardly the point, is it?

Sincerely

T Ravenscroft (Mr)

AB WORLD FOODS

**Consumer Services**
**Kingsmill Place**
**Vauxhall Road**
**Maidenhead**
**SL6 4UF**

Ref: 4409193

Mr T Ravenscroft
19 Victoria Gardens
New Mills
High Peak
SK12 4BC

Dear Mr Ravenscroft

Thank you very much for taking the trouble to write with your comments about our Pataks products.

We here at AB World Foods always welcome feedback of either a positive or negative nature.

I have passed your comments on to our Marketing Department, as I know how much they value customer opinions.

Please find enclosed vouchers to the value of £3, which we would like you to accept to go towards your next purchase

Yours sincerely,

Luke Chapman
Customer Services Advisor

19 Victoria Gardens
New Mills
High Peak
SK12 4BC

6th February 2015

Luke Chapman
Consumer Services
A B World Foods
Vauxhall Road
Maidenhead
SL6 4UF

Ref: 4409193

Dear Luke Chapman

So Pataks isn't Pataks now, it's really A B Foods. Is that another of their secrets?

With the £3 voucher I bought a jar of your Madras Curry Sauce. I couldn't fault it, although for all I know it could have been Vindaloo mixed half and half with Jalfrezi if your past cavalier approach to cooking is any indication.

Sincerely

T Ravenscroft (Mr)

****

19 Victoria Gardens
New Mills
High Peak
SK12 4BC

6th Febuary 2015

Customer Care
The Rainforest Café
20 Shaftesbury Avenue
London
W1D 7EU

Dear Rainforest Café

On a trip to London on the 2nd February my wife and I, both keen environmentalists and David Attenborough aficionados, took the opportunity of dining at your well-regarded café. For our 'Before the Adventure' dish we both chose your Raging Thunder Buffalo Wings. For our 'The Adventure Begins' dish my wife chose Major Mojo Bones, whilst I went for Volcanic Chilli Con Carne. After two generously portioned courses we had both eaten quite sufficient so didn't enquire if you had a 'The Adventure Ends' desserts menu. However *my* adventure ended at about three-o-clock the following morning when I woke up with an attack of the runs.

We had both had Raging Thunder Buffalo Wings, my wife was unaffected by her Major Mojo Bones, so the problem could only have been the Volcanic Chilli Con Carne, which proved to be a volcanic concoction in more ways than one, as about two dozen trips to the lavatory over the course of the next forty eight hours would bear testimony. I don't wonder you call it Volcanic judging from the eruptions from my bottom it occasioned.

Has anyone else complained of being similarly inconvenienced after eating your Volcanic Chilli Con Carne?

Sincerely

T Ravenscroft (Mr)

A WILD PLACE TO SHOP AND EAT ®

Monday 16th Feb 2015

Dear Mr Ravenscroft

Further to your letter, we are sorry to hear that your wife was feeling unwell following your recent visit. I hasten to add that comments of this nature are taken seriously.

Currently we have not received any other calls of this nature relating to any menu item on the day of your visit but we will continue to monitor calls for other comments of a similar nature. For your reference 6 Volcanic Chilli Con Carnes were sold on the 2nd Feb 2015.

Without having extensive tests done by your Doctor it is impossible to conclusively confirm that it was indeed the meal that caused the sickness but would thank you again for bringing it to my attention as without question I understand your concerns.

Taking into account the aforementioned I would also respectfully highlight that without tests being carried out the symptoms could equally have been triggered by a viral bug as opposed to alleged food poisoning. We hope your wife is feeling better and please feel free to contact us once your doctor has more conclusive results.

Kind Regards

Nikola Rogic
Assistant General Manager
Rainforest Café, London.

**20 Shaftesbury Avenue, Piccadilly Circus, London, W1D 7EU**

19 Victoria Gardens
New Mills
High Peak
SK12 4BC

18th February 2015

Nikola Rogic
The Rainforest Café
20 Shaftesbury Avenue
London
W1D 7EU

Dear Nikola Rogic

You are probably correct in your contention that it was a viral bug that did the damage. However I would feel a little more assured of this had you gleaned from my letter that it was me who got the runs, not my wife. And if you got that wrong, well....

You will no doubt be pleased to learn that I am now fit and well again. Not only that, I plan to visit your café again early next month. In fact your assurance that no other complaints resulted from the sale of the 6 Volcanic Chilli Con Carnes that day has mollified me to such an extent that I will be trying the dish once more, as it was a lot nicer going in than it was coming out. However, and in view of what followed the last time I had it, I suggest that a complimentary meal might be in order, if not a complimentary bucket.

Sincerely

T Ravenscroft (Mr)

Rainforest Cafe

A WILD PLACE TO SHOP AND EAT ®

Monday 23rd February 2015

Dear Mr Ravenscroft

Further to our recent correspondence, I wanted to write to you to convey my sympathies to you regarding your recent illness and I hope you are feeling better. I am confident that your sickness did not originate from the Rainforest Café and can confirm to date we have received no additional communication relating to further instances of a similar nature.

That said, I would welcome an opportunity to invite you and your guests back to the Rainforest Café London to restore your faith in us. As a gesture of goodwill please find a voucher for £25 (twenty five pounds), to be used as full or part payment on your next visit.

To ensure the visit gets off to an excellent start, please contact Frankie Mae in my Sales and Marketing team on 020 7434 3111 so that she can book you the best available table for the size of your party.

We look forward to welcoming you back to the restaurant.

Yours Sincerely

Nikola Rogic
Assistant General Manager
Rainforest Café, London.

**20 Shaftesbury Avenue, Piccadilly Circus, London, W1D 7EU**

19 Victoria Gardens
New Mills
High Peak
SK12 4BC
SK22 4LL

26th February 2015

Nikola Rogic
The Rainforest Café
20 Shaftesbury Avenue
London
W1D 7EU

Dear Nikola Rogic

Thank you for the voucher for £25 (twenty five pounds). I would like a table near the lavatory.

Sincerely

T Ravenscroft (Mr)

****

19 Victoria Gardens
New Mills
High Peak
SK12 4BC

29th March 2015

Retail Customer Services
Marks & Spencer PLC
Chester Business Park
Wrexham Road
Chester
CH4 9GA

Dear Marks and Spencer

One day, whilst on holiday in Spain, a man forsook the lure of the beach in favour of a walk in the countryside. Soon he came across a peasant. Cradled in the peasant's hands was a one-legged chicken. "How did your chicken lose its leg," the holidaymaker asked.

The peasant smiled and patted the chicken affectionately on the head. "This chicken - he is called Severiano - this chicken is the bravest chicken in all of Spain. Two months ago I was swimming in the sea. Half a mile from the shore I caught cramp. Sitting on the beach waiting for me, Severiano saw me struggling. With no regard for his own safety he flew out to me as fast as he could bat his little wings, and just as I was going down for the third time he grabbed hold of my swimming trunks with his beak and towed me to safety."

"That's most impressive," said the holidaymaker. "But how did it lose its leg?"

"One month ago," said the peasant, "I was coming home late at night when I was set upon by three robbers. They said they would beat me to death if I didn't give them money. I told them I was a poor peasant, I had no money. They started to beat me to death. From his chicken coop at my humble adobe a mile away my brave Severiano heard my cries for help. With a single bound he escaped from the coop and flew at a hundred miles an hour to my assistance. Reaching the scene of the crime he rose a hundred feet in the air and dive-bombed at the three robbers and pecked each of them with his beak...peck, peck, peck, peck, peck! The robbers fled."

"That's some chicken you have there," said the holidaymaker. "But how did it lose its leg?"

"Last week," said the peasant, "I was out walking in the mountains with my brave Severiano. Suddenly I slipped and lost my footing. I fell over the edge of a cliff into a five hundred feet deep ravine. I was only about five feet from the bottom of the ravine when my chicken, my brave Severiano, with no regard for his own safety, flew down the cliff at the speed of sound, grabbed my shirt in his little beak, and flew with me back up the cliff face to safety."

"That's marvellous, it really is," said the holidaymaker. "But you still haven't explained why it lost its leg."

The peasant smiled and stroked the chicken affectionately. "Well," he said, "when you have a chicken as brave as Severiano you don't eat it all at once."

I was reminded of the above story yesterday after purchasing one of your organic, free range, class A, British whole chickens, only to find on getting it home and unpacking it that, like the Spanish peasant's chicken, it had only one leg. Well actually it had one leg and one thigh, the drumstick part of its other leg being absent. In all fairness I would point out that the weight stated on the packing, 2.1kg, was accurate - I checked it on my kitchen scales - so whoever packed it was probably aware that it was minus part of a leg (otherwise it would have weighed more, to the amount of the weight of a drumstick).

Would you care to comment as I wouldn't expect to find fault with a Marks & Spencer organic, free range, class A, British whole chicken, a chicken that I have bought many times in the past without cause for complaint.

Sincerely

T Ravenscroft (Mr)

MARKS & SPENCER

Retail Customer Services
Chester Business Park
Wrexham Road
Chester
CH4 9GA

Mr Terence Ravenscroft
19 Victoria Gardens
New Mills
High Peak
SK12 4BC

Our Ref: 116028
8 April 2015

Dear Mr Ravenscroft

Thank you very much for your letter regarding the British organic chicken you've bought from us recently.

I'm very sorry to hear it only had one leg and thigh, I appreciate this must have been disappointing for you and it's certainly concerning to hear.

I've looked into this for you, and in our experience we've found this very rarely happens, but can sometimes occur during the manufacturing process.

We have rigorous control agreements with all of our food suppliers to ensure our food products meet the highest possible standard of quality. So it's concerning to hear this hasn't been the case on this occasion.

However I have reported this matter to our Food Technologist and our supplier. They will look into what has gone wrong and will take steps to improve this product in the future, and prevent this happening again.

All the details are now on our system, which we use to closely monitor the performance of each supplier. I assure you our food technologists will take action if we feel the highest quality standards aren't being kept.

I've also arranged for a GiftCard to be sent to you as a gesture of goodwill, which I hope you'll be happy to accept with our sincere apologies and best wishes. I do hesitate to contact us hope you can enjoy spending it online or in our stores.

Thank you very much for bringing this to our attention. Please don't hesitate to contact us if you have any further queries.

Yours sincerely

Kelly Melia<br>
Retail Customer Services.

19 Victoria Gardens
New Mills
High Peak
SK12 4BC

13th April 2015

Retail Customer Services
Marks & Spencer PLC
Chester Business Park
Wrexham Road
Chester
CH4 9GA

Dear Kelly Melia

Thank you for the £15 GiftCard. I gave it to my wife with instructions to buy another of your organic chickens and to spend the balance on something for herself. She said she would probably buy a pair of tights. It occurred to me that if your quality control people can miss spotting a one-legged chicken then they wouldn't have too much trouble letting a pair of one-legged tights escape their attention, so advised her to satisfy herself that the tights had two legs before parting with the GiftCard. It gives me pleasure to inform you that both the chicken and the tights had a full complement of legs.

Something has suggested itself to me since my initial letter. The white meat of a chicken is generally more highly regarded than the dark meat, a fact reflected in the comparative prices of breast meat and leg meat when buying them separately. So when I purchased the one-legged chicken from you I was in fact getting something of a bargain, as I was getting a higher ratio of white meat to dark for the same price as a two-legged bird. Bearing this in mind it occurred to me that if Marks and Spencer were to breed chickens with only one leg, or even better, no legs at all, they would make better profits than they do with two-legged chickens. I suppose you would get the RSPCA moaning that a chicken with no legs wouldn't be able to walk, and this would be true, but battery chickens don't get to walk very much as things are, and although the same thing can't be said for free-range chickens, where are you going to go if you're a chicken? To the pub? I mean an absence of legs isn't going to interfere with their social life, is it? It's not as though it will stop them going to the cinema or a football match or the Pyramid Stage at Glastonbury to watch the Kings of Leon.

I would like to take this idea further, as I think it is a belter. Could you direct me to the relevant department that deals with such matters, and perhaps the name of the person to write to?

Sincerely

T Ravenscroft (Mr)

MARKS & SPENCER

Retail Customer Services
Chester Business Park
Wrexham Road
Chester
CH4 9GA

Mr Terence Ravenscroft
19 Victoria Gardens
New Mills
High Peak
SK12 4BC

Our Ref: 116028
16 April 2015

Dear Mr Ravenscroft

Thank you for your further letter. I'm glad to hear your wife has been able to enjoy the gift card I sent you, and it's great to hear her tights were our usual high quality.

With regards to your proposal, it would be our department that you would contact. I've recorded your comments on our system for the attention of our Food Team, they look after proposals and suggestions from customers.

I'm afraid they're not a customer facing department so you won't receive any feedback unless they decide to go ahead with the idea.

Thanks again for bringing this to our attention, if we can be of any further assistance please don't hesitate to get in touch.

Yours sincerely

Kelly Melia
Retail Customer Services.

19 Victoria Gardens
New Mills
High Peak
SK12 4BC

20th April 2015

Retail Customer Services
Marks & Spencer PLC
Chester Business Park
Wrexham Road
Chester
CH4 9GA

Dear Kelly

By sheer coincidence no sooner had I received your letter than I got an email from M&S offering me '20% off 'selected Womenswear, Lingerie, Beauty, Menswear, Kidswear, Homeware, Hampers and Selected Flowers. Sadly, there was no mention of chickens. However it occurred to me that should your Food Team take up my idea of breeding legless chickens (in other words, chickens that are about 20% less than normal chickens), that '20% Off' would be an excellent slogan with which to promote them, as it would be nothing less than the truth whilst at the same time allowing you to legitimately charge the usual price. Not for one moment that I am suggesting a reputable company like Marks &Spencer would stoop to such underhand tactics. But then I didn't think Mars would stoop to reducing the size of their Mars Bars, twice, whilst still charging the same price, so you never know.

Sincerely

T Ravenscroft (Mr)

PS. The tights are still going strong.

****

So what's all this then - a book called Dear Pepsi-Cola with no letters to and from Pepsi-Cola in it? Well in fact I wrote to Pepsi twice. Sadly, twice they didn't bother to reply. Whether or not this suggests that the Coca-Cola Company, who answered my letters promptly and with concern when I wrote to them, cares more for its customers than does Pepsi-Cola, I couldn't possibly comment.